Theodore Henry Hittell

Brief History of California

Theodore Henry Hittell

Brief History of California

ISBN/EAN: 9783337375102

Printed in Europe, USA, Canada, Australia, Japan

Cover: Foto ©ninafisch / pixelio.de

More available books at **www.hansebooks.com**

BRIEF HISTORY

OF

CALIFORNIA

BY

THEODORE H. HITTELL

———

With an Introduction and Suggestive Correlations by
RICHARD D. FAULKNER,
PRINCIPAL FRANKLIN GRAMMAR SCHOOL, SAN FRANCISCO, CALIFORNIA

Maps, Portraits and Other Illustrations
BY
CHARLES J. HITTELL

———

BOOK I

— -

THE STONE EDUCATIONAL COMPANY
SAN FRANCISCO
1898

INTRODUCTION.

BY RICHARD D. FAULKNER.

The history of California is unique. Its periods of growth are distinct epochs. It did not grow out of complex situations. A series of logical events succeeded each other, apparently in natural sequence, until a typical State of the United States was completely evolved. Its history since its admission is equal in interest to its romantic past and its thrilling present.

A study of the history of such a State can not fail to interest, instruct, and inspire its future citizens.

The early history of the State, being the narrative of explorations in which the motive of the explorers is readily perceived, serves as an admirable introduction to the history of the United States, with which it is closely correlated. Its study can therefore be introduced early into the course of the elementary schools, and if completed, it will be an excellent preparation for a survey in the secondary schools of the whole history of the American continent.

It was difficult, until Mr. Theodore H. Hittell in 1897 completed his "History of California" in four volumes, to give to the pupils of the public schools a conception of the history of the State, without great labor on the part of the teacher; but it was generally recognized by teachers that the completion of this work made it possible to do so with the minimum of expense in time and effort. But to further minimize time and effort on the part of teachers, and at the same time to give pupils an opportunity of acquiring for themselves directly some knowledge of the history of the State, the author of the "History of California" has written, with all his charm of style and historical accuracy, a "Brief History of California" that can be read and comprehended by the pupils of the grammar grades of the public schools.

In the "History of California," the history of the State is discussed in twelve subdivisions termed books, the titles of which

(iii)

are: Early Voyages, The Jesuits, The Franciscans, The Spanish
Governors, The Mexican Governors, The Last Mexican Gov-
ernors, The Americans, Early Mining Times, Progress of San
Francisco, State Growth, Early State Administrations, Later
State Administrations.

The plan of the "Brief History of California" is substan-
tially that of the "History of California," and in many cases the
same language is used. It consists of twelve subdivisions or
books—the titles, however, differing slightly from those of the
larger work. It is to be published in three forms: First, each
subdivision or book under its own title, as each, though an
integral part of the whole, is complete within itself; second, in
parts, a part consisting of three of its subdivisions or books;
third, in a single volume.

It is designed as a text-book for instruction in the history
of the State and for supplementary reading.

It is believed that provision can be made for its use in
schools, with but slight revision of Courses of Study, as it
correlates closely on the one hand with the history of each
pupil's neighborhood and on the other with the "History of the
United States."

It is thought that the time required for instruction in local
and State history will be more than offset by the alertness
of mind which it will produce in awakening the interest of
the pupils in their immediate surroundings, and in the past,
present, and future of not only the section in which they live,
but of the State and of the great country of which it is a part.

It is suggested that Part I be introduced into the sixth
grade, Part II into the seventh, Part III into the eighth and
Part IV into the ninth. But this is only a suggestion. It is
expected that Boards of Education will exercise their discretion
in its grading. The plan of its publication is intended to give
flexibility to its introduction into the schools.

The maps, portraits, and other illustrations of the "Brief
History of California" are carefully drawn by Mr. Charles J.
Hittell from the most authentic sources, and may be relied
upon as correct. It is the aim that they shall be educative
within themselves, not only as suggestive of sources of information but also from an artistic standpoint.

August 4, 1898.

CONTENTS.

BOOK I.

DISCOVERY AND EARLY VOYAGES.

CHAPTER I.

AMERICA AND INDIA.

CHAPTER II.

CORTES AND CALIFORNIA.

CHAPTER III.

THE SEVEN CITIES OF CIBOLA.

(v)

CHAPTER IV.

CORONADO AND ALARCON.

CHAPTER V.

CABRILLO.

CHAPTER VI.

THE PHILIPPINE TRADE.

CHAPTER X.

VISCAINO.

CHAPTER XI.

THE PEARL FISHERS.

CHAPTER XII.

ADMIRAL ATONDO.

MAPS, PORTRAITS AND OTHER ILLUSTRATIONS.

(ix)

PRONOUNCING VOCABULARY.

[It is deemed proper, on account chiefly of the many Spanish names adopted and used in California, to give a pronouncing vocabulary of the principal words. As a preliminary it may be briefly stated that in Spanish the vowels always have the same sound and are pronounced as follows:

a like ah, or a in far;   e like ay in may;
i like ee in see;   o like oh, or o in no;
u like oo in food;   y, when a vowel, like ee.
Final e is always sounded.

Of the consonants; c before e or i is sounded like th in thin, though some prefer the sound of s; before a, o or u and before consonants, it is pronounced like k; ch like ch in chair or church.

g before e or i is pronounced like h; in other cases, like g in game.

h is silent; hua is pronounced like wa in water.

ll has the sound of lli in million and

ñ the sound of ni in minion.

q is always followed by u and another vowel and has the sound of k (the u being silent).

s has the hissing sound like ss and never the z sound, which is not used in Spanish.

z is pronounced like th, though some prefer the sound of s.

Special attention is called to the accent ', which is always strong.]

Acapulco—*Ah-cah-pool'-koh.*
Acus—*Ah'-koos.*
Aguada Segura (safe watering-port) — *Ag-wah'-dah Say-goo'-rah.*
Aguilar, Martin de—*Mahr-teen' day Ah-ghee-lahr'.*

Alarcon, Hernando de — *Ayr-nahn'-doh day Ah-lar-kohn'.*
Alvarado, Pedro de—*Pay'-droh day Ahl-vah-rah'-doh.*
Anian—*Ahn-yahn'.*
Año Nuevo (new year)—*Ahn'-yoh Noo-ay'-voh.*

(xi)

Apostolos Valerianus—*Ah-post'-
o-los Vah-layr-ee-ahn'-us.*
Arica—*Ah-ree'-kah.*
Atondo y Antillon, Isidro—
*Ecss'-ee-droh Ah-tohn'-doh ee
Ahn-teel-yohn'.*

Badajoz—*Bah-dah-hohth'.*
Balboa, Vasco Nuñez de —
*Vahss'-koh Noon'-yayth day
Bahl-boh'-ah.*
Becerra de Mendoza, Diego —
*Dec-ay'-goh Bay-thayr'-rah day
Mayn-doh'-thah.*
Bigonia—*Bee-gohn'-yah.*
Blanco (white)—*Blahn'-koh.*
Buena Guia (good guide) —
Bway'-nah Ghee'-ah.

Cabeza de Vaca, Alvar Nuñez—
*Ahl-vahr' Noon'-yayth Kah-
bay'-thah day Vah'-kah.*
Cabo Bajo (low cape)—*Kah'-
boh Bah'-hoh.*
Cabo del Engaño—*Kah'-boh del
Ayn-gahn'-yoh.*
Cabrillo, Juan Rodriguez —
*Whaen Rohd-ree'-gayth Kah-
breel'-yoh.*
Cacafuego— *Kah-kah-fway'-goh.*
Canoas, Pueblo de las (town
of the canoes)—*Pwayb'-loh
day lahss Kah-noh'-ahss.*
Carboneli, Estevan —*Ayss-tay'-
vahn, Kahr-boh-nay'-lee.*
Casanate, Pedro Portel de—
*Pay'-droh Pohr-tayl' day Kah-
sah-nah'-tay.*
Castillo, Domingo del—*Doh-
meen'-yoh del Kahss-teel'-yoh.*
Cavendish — *Cav'-en-dish;* by
some pronounced *Kan'-dish.*

Cedros (cedars) — *Thay'-drohss.*
Cermeñon, Sebastian Rodriguez
—*Say-bahsst-yahn' Rohd-ree'-
gayth Thayr-mayn-yohn'.*
Cerros (hills)—*Thayr'-rohss.*
Chile—*Tchee'-lay,* but by some
pronounced *Chil'-lee.*
Cíbola—*Theeb'-oh-lah;* by some
pronounced *Seeb'-oh-lah.*
Colorado (red) — *Koh-loh-rah'-
doh.*
Concepcion — *Kohn-thayp-thee-
ohn'.*
Coras—*Koh'-rahss.*
Coronado, Francisco Vasquez
de — *Fran-theess'-koh Vahss'-
kayss day Koh-roh-nah'-doh.*
Cortereal, Gaspar—*Gahss-pahr'
Kor-tay-ray-ahl'.*
Cortés, Hernando — *Ayr-nahn'-
doh Kor-tayss'.*
Culiacan—*Koo-lee-ah-kahn'.*

Darien—*Dah-ree-ayn'.*
Defoe—*Dee-foh'.*
De Verde—*Day Vayr'-day.*

Ecuador—*Ay-kwah-dohr'.*
El Dorado—*Ayl Doh-rah'-doh.*
Engaño, Cabo del (cape of deceit)—*Kah'-boh del Ayn-gahn'-
yoh.*
Escalona, Luis de — *Loo-eess'
day Ayss-kah-loh'-nah.*
Estevanico — *Ayss-tay-vahn-ee'-
koh.*

Ferrelo Bartolomé—*Bahr-tohl-
oh-may' Fayr-ray'-loh.*
Fuca, Juan de — *Whaen day
Foo'-kah.*

Gali, Francisco — *Fran-theess'-koh Gah'-lee.*

Gallápagos — *Gahl-yahp'-ah-gohss;* by some pronounced *Gahl-yah-pay'-gus.*

Gicamas—*Hee-kah'-mahss.*

Grande, Rio (great river)— *Ree'-oh Grahn'-day.*

Grixalva, Hernando de—*Ayr-nahn'-doh day Gree-hahl'-vah.*

Guatemala — *Gwah-tay-mah'-lah.*

Guatulco—*Gwah-tool'-koh.*

Guayaquil—*Gwy-ah-keel'.*

Guaycuros—*Gwy-koor'-ohss.*

Guaymas—*Gwy'-mahss.*

Herodotus—*He-rod'-o-tus.*

Hurtado de Mendoza — *Oohr-tah'-doh day Mayn-doh'-thah.*

Ibimuhueite— *Ee-bee-moo-hway-ee'-tay.*

Islas de Poniente (islands of the setting sun) —*Ecss'-lahss day Poh-nee-ayn'-tay.*

Iturbi, Juan—*Whawn Ee-toor'-bee.*

Jalisco—*Hah-lees'-koh.*

Java—*Hah'-vah.*

Juan de Fuca — *Whawn day Foo'-kah.*

Juan Fernandez—*Whawn Fayr-nahn'-dayth.*

Kühn—*Keen.*

Kino, Eusebio Francisco—*Oo-sayb'-yoh Fran-theess'-koh Kee'-noh.*

Ladrillero, Juan Fernandez— *Whawn Fayr-nahn'-dayth day Lah-dreel-yay'-roh,*

Ladrones (robbers) — *Lah-drohn'-ayss.*

La Paz (peace)—*Lan Pahth.*

Las Virgines (the virgins)— *Lahss Veer'-hee-nayss.*

Legaspi, Miguel Lopez de— *Mee-gayl' Loh'-payth day Lay-gahss'-pee.*

Lemaire—*Lay-mayr'.*

Loma (hill)—*Loh'-mah.*

Loreto—*Loh-ray'-toh.*

Luzenilla, Francisco — *Fran-theess'-koh Loo-thay-neel'-yah.*

Madrid—*Mad-reed'.*

Magdalena— *Mahg-dah-lay'-nah.*

Magellan, Fernando — *Fayr-nahn'-doh Mah-hayl-yahn';* by some pronounced *May-gel'-lan.*

Maldonado, Lorenzo Ferrer de — *Loh-rayn'-thoh Fayr-rayr' day Mahl-doh-nah'-doh.*

Maldonado, Pedro Nuñez — *Pay'-droh Noon'-yayth Mahl-doh-nah'-doh.*

Marata—*Mah-rah'-tah.*

Mayo—*My'-oh.*

Mazatlan—*Mah-that-lahn'.*

Mazuela, Juan de—*Whawn day Mah-thway'-lah.*

Mendocino — *Mayn-doh-theen'-oh.*

Mendoza, Antonio de—*Ahn-tohn'-yoh day Mayn-doh'-thah.*

Mendoza, Diego Becerra de— *Dee-ay'-goh Bay-thayr'-rah day Mayn-doh'-thah.*

Mendoza, Hurtado de—*Oohr-tah'-doh day Mayn-doh'-thah.*

Monterey—*Mon-tay-ray'.*

Narvaez, Panfilo de—*Pahn'-fec-loh day Nahr-vah'-ayth.*

Navidad (nativity) — *Nah-vee-dah á'.*

Newfoundland— *Noo'-fund-land.*

Nieve (snow)—*Nee-ay'-vay.*

Niza, Marcos de—*Mahr'-kohss day Nee'-thah.*

Nuestra Señora de la Incarnacion y .Desengaño (Our Lady of the Incarnation and Undeceit) — *Noo-ayss'-trah Sayn-yoh'-rah day lah Een-kahr-nah-thee-ohn' ee Day-sayn-gahn'-yoh.*

Ortega, Francisco de—*Fran-theess'-koh day Ohr-tay'-gah.*

Padilla, Juan de—*Whawn day Pah-deel'-yah.*

Panama—*Pah-nah-mah'.*

Payta—*Py'-tah.*

Peru—*Pay-roo'.*

Philippiue—*Phil-ip-peen'.*

Pichilingue—*Pee-cheel-een'-gay.*

Piñadero, Bernardo Bernal de —*Bayr-nahr'-doh Bayr-nahl' day Peen-yah-day'-roh.*

Pinos (pines)—*Pee'-nohss.*

Poniente, Islas de (isles of the setting sun)—*Ecss'-lahss day Poh-nee-ayn'-tay.*

Posesion (possession) — *Poh-sayss-yohn'.*

Pueblo de las Canoas (town of the canoes)—*Pwayb'-loh day lahss Kah-noh'-ahss.*

Pueblos (towns)—*Pwayb'-lohss.*

Puerto Seguro (secure port)— *Pwayr'-toh Say-goo'-roh.*

Quivira—*Kee-vee'-rah.*

Reyes (kings)—*Ray'-ayss.*

Rio Grande (great river)— *Ree'-oh Grahn'-day.*

Rogers, Woodes—*Woodz Rog'-ers.*

San Agustin — *Sahn Ah-goos-teen'.*

San Bernabé—*Sahn Bayr-nah-bay'.*

San Bruno—*Sahn Broo'-noh.*

San Clemente — *Sahn Clay-mayn'-tay.*

San Diego—*Sahn Dee-ay'-goh.*

Sandoval, Gonzalo de—*Gohn-thah'-loh day Sahn-doh-vahl'.*

San Gerónimo—*Sahn Hay-rohn'-ee-moh.*

San José del Cabo—*Sahn Hoh-say' dayl Kah'-boh.*

San Juan Capistrano—*Sahn Whawn Kap-pees-trah'-noh.*

San Lucas—*Sahn Loo'-kahss.*

San Miguel—*Sahn Mee-gayl'.*

San Salvador—*Sahn Sahl-vah-dohr'.*

Santa Ana—*Sahn'-tah Ahn'-nah.*

Santa Barbara — *Sahn'-tah Bahr'-bah-rah.*

Santa Catalina—*Sahn'-tah Kah-tah-lee'-nah.*

Santa Cruz—*Sahn'-tah Krooth;* by some pronounced *Kroos.*

Santa Rosa—*Sahn'-tah Roh'-sah.*

Santos, Todos los (all the saints) — *Toh'-dohss lohss Sahn'-tohss.*

Santo Tomas—*Sahn'-toh Toh-mahss'.*

Sardinas (sardines)—*Sahr-dee'-nahss.*

Sejo—*Say'-hoh.*

Seville—*Say-veel'-yay;* in English usually pronounced *Say'-veel* or *Say-veel'.*

Sinaloa—*Seen-ah-loh'-ah.*

Shelvocke—*Shel'-vok.*

Sonora—*Soh-noh'-rah.*

St. Julien—*Sahng Jool-yahng'.*

Tatarrax—*Tah-tahr-rax'.*

Tehuantepec — *Tay-whawn'-tay-payk.*

Ternate—*Tayr-nah'-tay.*

Tidore—*Tee-doh'-ray.*

Todos los Santos (all the saints) — *Toh'-dohss lohss Sahn'-tohss.*

Totonteac—*To-tohn-tay-ak'.*

Ulloa, Francisco de — *Frantheess'-koh day Ool-yoh'-ah.*

Urdaneta, Andres de—*Ahn-drayss' day Oor-dah-nay'-tah.*

Vaca, Alvar Nuñez Cabeza de—*Ahl-vahr' Noon'-yayth Kah-bay'-thah day Vah'-kah.*

Valerianus, Apostolos — *Ah-post'-o-los Vah-layr-ee-ahn'-us.*

Valparaiso—*Vaht-pah-ry'-soh.*

Van Shouten—*Fahn Shoot'-en.*

Verde, De—*Day Vayr'-day.*

Victoria (victory)—*Veek-tohr'-yah.*

Virgines, Las (the virgins)— *Lahss Veer'-hee-nayss.*

Viscaino, Sebastian — *Say-bahsst-yahn' Veess-ky'-noh.*

Woodes Rogers—*Woodz Rog'-ers.*

Ximenez, Fortuño—*Fohr-toon'-yoh Hee-may'-nayth.*

Zacatula—*Tha-kah-too'-lah.*

Zuñi—*Thoon'-yee.*

Zuñiga, Gaspar de, Conde de Monterey — *Gahss-pahr' day Thoon-yee'-gah, Kohn'-day day Mon-tay-ray'.*

BRIEF HISTORY OF CALIFORNIA.

BOOK I.

Discovery and Early Voyages.

CHAPTER I.

AMERICA AND INDIA.

To understand the circumstances under which California was discovered, and therefore how its history commences, it is necessary to go back to the time of Christopher Columbus. It must be recollected that, when he undertook his famous voyage in 1492, he was in search of a western route to Asia; and that, when he discovered America, he supposed he had reached India. It was for this reason that he called the natives of the new land Indians—a name which was soon applied to all the aborigines of America. It was also for the same reason that the islands he found afterwards got to be called the West Indies, to distinguish them from the East Indies. As a matter of fact, the natives of America were no more like the natives of India than they were like the Spaniards; and, as for the West Indies, they were at least three thousand miles further away from India than Spain, whence Columbus had sailed.

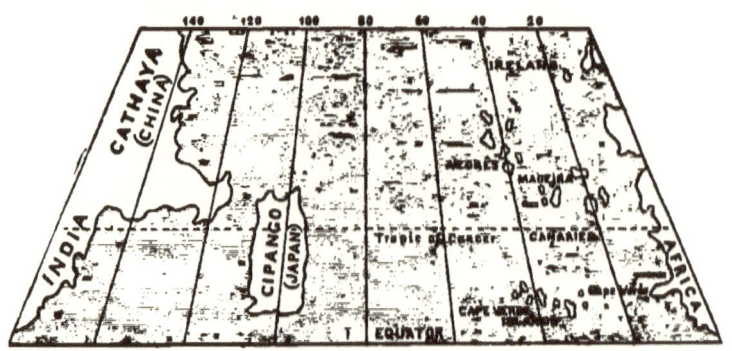

TOSCANELLI'S MAP OF 1474.
[Used by Columbus on his first voyage.]

But this belief—that India had been reached—though a great mistake, was of immense importance and had far-reaching consequences. From the earliest ages, India had always been regarded as a land of unlimited wealth. Herodotus, the so-called father of history, who wrote nearly five hundred years before the Christian era, spoke in glowing terms about it and particularly of its production of gold, which he represented as guarded by large and savage ants and fierce, fire-breathing griffins. It is probable that this fanciful and seemingly absurd story originated in the simple circumstance that the gold mines of India were worked by warlike tribes of men, who were as laborious as ants, and that, to reach them, deserts had to be crossed, which were as hot as the supposed scorching breath of griffins. However this may have been, it is certain that the old stories of the riches and greatness of India, thus started in the far distant past, grew and expanded as time passed on; and that, in the days of Columbus and his successors, the most extravagant notions were entertained, not only about its gold, but also about its silks and spices, its rare gems and costly gums, the magnificence of its princes, the grandeur of its courts, the extent of its kingdoms, and the countless number of its people.

THE SHIPS OF COLUMBUS.

[From models exhibited at World's Columbian Exposition, Chicago, 1893.]

It was this idea of the marvelous, treasure-bearing countries of India, lying open to conquest, that induced the Spaniards, after discovering the West India Islands and finding in them little of the wealth they expected, to persist, at great labor and expense, in carrying their explorations further and further. They still regarded the lands they had found as portions of India, though poor portions, and believed that the rich portions could not be far beyond. Accordingly, when Vasco Nuñez de Balboa in 1513 crossed over the Isthmus of Darien and discovered a great ocean, he supposed it the sea that was known to wash the southern shores of India; and he therefore called it the South Sea. This again was a great mistake; for, instead of being the sea washing the southern shores of India, it was the largest and grandest ocean on the globe; and it could no more properly be called the South Sea—though it continued for many years to be known as such—than the Atlantic Ocean could properly be called the North Sea.

In 1520, when Fernando Magellan discovered the straits that bear his name and sailed through them into the vast expanse of waters to the west, he recognized it as a new and great ocean; and, on account of its calmness and smoothness in comparison with the storm-vexed Atlantic, he called it the Pacific. He not only recognized and gave it a proper name; but he also sailed for many thousand miles across its broad bosom, and in 1521 discovered the Philippine Islands, which were in reality a part of the Indies that Columbus supposed he had reached in 1492. But, notwithstanding Magellan's discovery that the real Indies, of which such magnificent and attractive accounts had been told, were at least ten thousand miles from America, still the Spaniards thought that the two countries stretched out towards, and abutted upon, each other; that all the northern parts of the Pacific Ocean were dry land, and that all the regions between America and India, if not properly parts of India, were at any rate quite as rich and populous.

SUGGESTIVE CORRELATIONS.

TO THE TEACHER.

The question—Why was Columbus in search of a western passage to Asia?—naturally suggests itself on the reading of the second sentence of Chapter 1 of this book.

It is presumed that the teacher will, preparatory to or in connection with the study of the chapter, discuss with the class the facts required for its proper answer.

The following questions involve the answer. If the subject, as outlined in them, is already familiar, they will serve for a review.

FOR THE PUPIL.

(To be studied with the Teacher.)

1. Name the three routes by ship and caravan over which the trade between Europe and Asia was carried on early in the fifteenth century.

    NOTE.—See map, Fiske's "History of the United States," p. 22, Gordy's "History of the United States," p. 4, or McMaster's "School History of the United States," p. 10.

2. What necessity arose for finding an ocean route to India?
3. When, by whom, and in what direction, was the first attempt made to find an ocean route?
4. In what particulars did the geographers, Ptolemy and Mela, disagree about the great continent that they both supposed existed south of the Equator?

    NOTE.—See maps, Fiske's "History of the United States," pp. 24-25.

5. Why did some inquiring minds shortly after 1471 begin to ask whether there could not possibly be a shorter route to India than around Africa?
6. What was the theory of Columbus about a shorter route?

TO THE PUPIL.

In not to exceed a half page of foolscap, written upon one side only, write three paragraphs upon The Discovery of America.

The paragraphs should contain answers to the questions below, which are the same as you have just studied, only restated in a different form.

Be careful that what you write be not merely a series of sentences answering the questions, but a plain and direct narrative which shall include their answer.

1. How and by what three routes was trade between Europe and Asia carried on early in the fifteenth century?
2. What necessity arose for finding an ocean route to Asia? And when, by whom, and in what direction, was the first attempt made to find such a route?
3. In what way, and about what time, did the difference of opinion between the geographers, Ptolemy and Mela,

influence the thought of the time to seek a route supposed
to be still shorter? What theory was advanced for such
a route, and who was its strongest advocate and first to
practically test it?

_____

REFERENCES.

TO THE TEACHER.

It is suggested, in connection with the thought contained
in this Chapter, that the class be given some idea of the condition of Europe before the discovery of America and some conception of the physical characteristics of the continent as
affecting historical development. Of course any presentation
of the subject should be in accordance with the age and grade
of the pupils.

In "A New History of the United States" by Horace E.
Scudder are two supplementary chapters, which discuss the
thoughts indicated. The titles of the chapters are:—

"The Preparation in Europe for the Discovery and Occupation of North America," and "The Physical Preparation of
North America for Occupation by European People."

A translation of the extant abridgment of the journal, kept
by Columbus on his first voyage, is Selection No. 17—"Discovery
of America"—in Hart's "American History told by Contemporaries," Vol. I.

A few references should be made to Sources. It is presumed the teacher will obtain and make use of such as
are proper correlations to the thought contained in the various
chapters.

The Topics—What are Sources, Educative Value of
Sources, Use of Sources by Teachers, Use of Sources by Pupils,
Cautions in Using Sources—are discussed in Hart's "American
History told by Contemporaries," Vol. I.

_____

SUGGESTIONS FOR ORAL DISCUSSION OR WRITTEN EXERCISES.

How America was taken for India, and why the Indians
were called Indians.

How and why the India-idea led to American explorations.

CHAPTER II.

CORTES AND CALIFORNIA.

GONZALO DE SANDOVAL.

[From "Das Alte Mexiko," by Th. Arnim, Leipzig, 1865.]

When Hernando Cortés conquered Mexico in 1521, he entertained the same idea that he was merely upon the threshold of India. When he found gold and silver in not inconsiderable quantities among the Aztecs, he felt justified in his belief in the greater wealth and barbaric splendor of the unknown regions beyond. And he was still more confirmed in this belief by a report, brought him by one of his lieutenants, named Gonzalo de Sandoval, in 1524, about an island lying at a distance of ten days' journey from the ocean coast west of Mexico, which was said to be inhabited by women only and to be very rich in pearls and gold. This strange story—which constitutes the first account of California that can be found in the old records—though it may be doubtful whether Cortés credited it in all its particulars, excited his imagination to such a degree that

he spent the next thirteen years of his life and almost all his
fortune in building ships and sending expeditions to search
out the supposed wonderful island, and in collecting and
finally leading a little army, and going in person to take possession of it.

The first of Cortés' ships that steered in the direction of
California was placed in charge of Pedro Nuñez Maldonado.
It sailed from Zacatula on the Pacific in 1528 and advanced
as far as the Santiago river in Jalisco. Cortés next,
in 1532, sent two ships, one in charge of Diego Hurtado de
Mendoza and the other in that of Juan de Mazuela. They
sailed from Acapulco and proceeded up along the coast as
far as the mouth of the Mayo river, where a mutiny
occurred, and Mazuela's ship was sent back with the mutineers. Hurtado proceeded further north and reached the
mouth of the Yaqui river, where he and his men were killed
by the Indians. ' The mutineers in Mazuela's ship met the
same fate on their way back along the coast of Jalisco.
Notwithstanding these misfortunes, Cortés sent two new
vessels from Tehuantepec in 1533. One was in charge of
Diego Becerra de Mendoza and the other in that of Hernando de Grixalva. They sailed only a short distance together and then separated. Grixalva ran out some distance
into the ocean and discovered the island of Santo Tomas, a
couple of hundred miles south of Cape San Lucas, but found
that it contained neither wealth nor human inhabitants.
Becerra de Mendoza, on the other hand, ran up the coast as
far as Jalisco, where a second mutiny broke out, which was
headed by Fortuño Ximenez, the chief pilot of the ship.
The mutineers, after killing Becerra, compelled his friends
to go ashore and then sailed with the vessel directly away
from the ill-fated coast. After being out of sight of land
for a number of days, they finally discovered what they supposed to be an island, but was in fact the place now known

NEW SPAIN

ILLUSTRATING EXPEDITIONS OF CORTES

as La Paz in Lower California. And thus it was that Cortés' mutinous pilot, Fortuño Ximenez, in 1534, became the discoverer of California.

Ximenez, as appears, disembarked on the supposed island and was there killed, with twenty of his companions, by the Indians. But a sufficient number of the sailors remained to navigate the vessel back to Jalisco, where they gave information of the discovery that had been made, and added that the supposed island was well peopled and that its coasts abounded in pearls. Cortés, as soon as he heard this report, notwithstanding the great losses he had sustained, immediately fitted out another expedition consisting of three ships, which sailed from Tehuantepec, and some four hundred persons with whom he embarked on the vessels at Chiametla in Jalisco; and, to insure faithful service, he put himself at the head of the adventurers. In May, 1535, he landed at the same place where Ximenez had been killed, and gave to it the name of Santa Cruz. He at once began investigations about the country; but it proved to be the most barren and forbidding he had ever beheld. There were a few natives, but they were the poorest, most abject, most degraded human creatures he had ever met. There were also some pearls along the shore, but not a particle of gold or silver or other wealth was to be seen.

In a very short time, on account of the failure of those whom he had ordered to follow him with further stores, his provisions ran low. His people began to suffer; and, when they began to suffer, they began to complain. He tried to console them with the promise of better times to come. He said that they had unfortunately struck a rough part of the country, but that further on they would undoubtedly find wealth and splendor enough to satisfy their most ardent longings. He also, as there is reason to believe, called their attention to the statements of a noted romance, published in

Spain in 1510, affirming the existence of an island, called California, which lay "on the right hand of the Indies, very near to the terrestrial paradise." It was said to be surrounded by steep rocks and almost inaccessible cliffs and to be peopled by women who lived the life of Amazons. These women were represented as of great bodily strength and courage; and it was added that their arms, as well as the trappings of the wild beasts, which they rode on their warlike expeditions, were entirely of gold—that being the only metal the island produced.

This story, which it will be noticed was in substance the same as that told by Sandoval in 1524, Cortés seems to have repeated to his suffering followers for the purpose of cheering up their spirits. He tried to make them believe that the barren rocks and cliffs they saw around them were only the surroundings of the wonderful island thus represented as lying close to the Indies and near the terrestrial paradise. However this may have been, it is certain that he supposed the country to be an island and that he gave to it the name, previously used in the romance referred to, of California. He himself believed it rich, and he made many attempts to explore it. But as far as he was able to penetrate, it continued to present the same rough and forbidding features. It was, in that part of it, a country of rocks and cliffs; its scant vegetation mostly thorny; its inhabitants poor, naked savages. There was no wealth and no indications of barbaric splendor. Under the circumstances, Cortés, in the beginning of 1537, feeling himself obliged to give up further search, returned, with most of his people, to Mexico; and he was soon afterwards followed by the remainder. And thus ended the first attempt of the Spaniards to settle California.

SUGGESTIVE CORRELATIONS.

TO THE TEACHER.

The natural outgrowth of the study of this Chapter and the succeeding one is the creation of an interest in the previous career of Cortés, or in other words, in the conquest of Mexico, and incidentally in the half-civilized tribes that existed not only in Mexico but elsewhere in America.

In the following detached sentences, the career of Cortés is traced from his birth until he scuttled and sunk his ships preparatory to his march on Mexico.

The pupil should be required to combine the detached statements into sentences, and the sentences into paragraphs. It is not necessary that the sentences be of one type. The sentence that will express clearly and directly the thought to be conveyed is the one to be used, whether it be simple, complex or compound. Of course long and involved sentences should be avoided. To get good results, it will be necessary to have the children write and rewrite. Criticise papers individually. Make free use of the blackboard. No effort shows quicker results than patient, painstaking work in English.

TO THE PUPIL.

The following detached statements are to be combined into sentences, and the sentences into paragraphs. The teacher will explain to you what you are required to do, and how it is to be done. Do the work so well that you will be prepared, when you have studied the succeeding chapter, to complete the story of The Conquest of Mexico in the order of the occurrence of the events, without reference to the book and without using the same expressions.

THE CONQUEST OF MEXICO.

Hernando Cortés was born in Medillin, Estremadura, Spain, in 1485. He came over to the West Indies in 1504. He served with distinction in the expedition sent in 1511 to conquer Cuba. The expedition was under command of Diego de Velasquez. It was sent from the island of Hispaniola. The Governor of Cuba, Velasquez, appointed him in the autumn of 1518 to command an important expedition fitted out for operations on the Mexican mainland. He was at that time Alcalde of Santiago de Cuba. Early in March, 1519, he landed at Tabasco on the southern shore of the Gulf of Campeachy. The natives were unfriendly and fought him. He defeated them. He seized a fresh stock of provisions. He proceeded to San Juan de Ulloa. From that place he sent messengers to Montezuma with gifts, and messages in the name of the king of Spain. He next founded Vera Cruz, a little to the north of its present site. He framed a municipal government for it. He then resigned his commission from Velasquez and was at once elected Captain-General by his municipality. He sent his flagship with influential and devoted friends to Spain to tell the king. He had his other ships scuttled and sunk.

1. What is the meaning of Alcalde?
2. Where is Santiago de Cuba?
3. Locate the following Mexican states: Tabasco, Vera Cruz, Puebla, Tlascala and Mexico.
4. What is the modern name for the island of Hispaniola?

THE EXPEDITIONS OF CORTES.

Complete the Table from the text of Chapters II and III.

NO.	EXPLORER.	SAILED FROM.	DATE.	HIGHEST POINT REACHED.	DIS-COVERED.
1.	Maldonado.				
2.	Hurtado. Mazuela.				
3.	Becerra. Ximenez. Grixalva.				
4.	Cortés.				
5.	Ulloa.			1. On Gulf of California? 2. Coast of Lower California?	1. What Port? 2. What Island?

CHAPTER III.

Cortés had scarcely reached Mexico on his return from California, when the whole country became exceedingly interested in reported new discoveries in the interior of the continent. In 1537 Alvar Nuñez Cabeza de Vaca and three companions, one of them a negro named Estevanico, made their appearance on the Pacific Coast and told a remarkable tale. They said that they belonged to an unfortunate expedition, which had in 1528 been conducted by Pánfilo de Narvaez into Florida; that their leader and all his comrades, except themselves, had lost their lives; that they had managed to escape and, by pretending to be great medicine-men and performing a number of cures among the Indians, had found means to subsist and pass from tribe to tribe; and that, after wandering a distance of more than three thousand miles and for a period of upwards of nine years, they had reached the Pacific and thence came to Mexico. They affirmed that they had seen bags of silver and arrow-heads of emerald in abundance, and that they had passed nations, and heard of others still further north, which possessed great cities and immense riches.

Cabeza de Vaca's narrative induced a Franciscan friar of Culiacan in Sinaloa, named Father Marcos de Niza, to visit the nations of the interior, thus said to be so wealthy. He accordingly, in 1539, set out, with a number of Indian companions, and taking along the negro Estevanico as his guide, traveled for several months northward into what is now New

Mexico. There he heard of a country called Cíbola, which contained seven great cities, lying close together and consisting of houses, several stories high, arranged in streets and having their portals adorned with turquoise stones. This news was brought him by messengers from Estevanico, who with most of the party had gone on in advance. As he traveled on, he heard more about the seven cities and their magnificence, and also about three other great kingdoms, called Marata, Acus and Totonteac. But unfortunately, just as he was about to reach Cíbola—which seems to have been the Zuñi country—he heard that Estevanico and all his companions had been seized by the inhabitants and put to death.

THE PUEBLO OF ZUNI.
[From photograph by Taber.]

On the reception of this sad intelligence, Father Marcos was of course afraid to approach any nearer; but, being unwilling to retrace his steps without at least a glimpse of the place, of which he had heard so much, he ascended the summit of a mountain and, looking down from it, beheld the famous cities in the distance. There were seven of them, as they had been described, lying not far apart, very similar to one another, consisting of high houses with flat roofs, seemingly built of stone and lime, and inhabited by a numerous and busy population. Being regularly laid out and white in color, they shone in the sunlight, so that the spectator had no difficulty in believing that their portals were adorned with precious stones. Upon getting back to the Spanish settlements, he sent to Mexico a description of all he had seen and a highly-colored account of all he had been told, adding also that the sea extended much further northward than was supposed and that there was a portion or arm of it not far from Cíbola.

The report of Father Marcos de Niza produced a fever of excitement throughout Mexico. Now, more than ever, it was supposed that all former discoveries and conquests in the new world would be cast in the shade, and that the dreams so long entertained of rich and populous nations— and it made little or no difference whether they were of India or some other country—would be realized. Not only was Cortés fully impressed with the general truth of all that was said and fully resolved to fit out a new expedition; but two rivals and competitors determined to do the same thing; for though Cortés had been named captain-general of New Spain, as Mexico was then called, and given the right to make discoveries and conquests in any other part of the new world, others claimed the same right. The first of these was Antonio de Mendoza, the viceroy, and the other was Pedro de Alvarado, a former lieutenant of Cortés, who was then governor of Guatemala.

There was no other man in New Spain to compare with Cortés in energy; and, long before his rivals could get ready, he prepared three ships and dispatched them for the new El Dorado. These he placed under the command of a trusted captain, named Francisco de Ulloa, who had been with him in California. His instructions were, as California was supposed to be an island and as Father Marcos de Niza had reported the sea or an arm of it to extend to the neighborhood of Cíbola, to sail in that direction and keep within sight of the mainland all the way. Ulloa accordingly sailed from Acapulco in July, 1539. He proceeded up the coast beyond the point previously reached and discovered the port, now known as Guaymas, where he landed and took possession of the country, as was usual on such occasions. Again embarking with two ships, for one had been lost on the way, he sailed still further up the coast and soon noticed that there was land on both sides east and west. After going more than a hundred leagues and passing several islands, he found that the mountains on each side began to approach nearer and nearer; that the sea became shoal, and that its waters, which had been clear, began to grow thick and muddy. He ascended to the mast-head of his ship and, seeing in the distant north that the lowlands from east and west stretched out towards each other, he satisfied himself that he could not advantageously sail any further in that direction.

Being determined to turn round, Ulloa first landed and took possession as before. He then ran down along what proved to be the eastern shore of Lower California. It soon became evident that he was in a gulf; but he hoped and expected to find an outlet, among the mountains on the west, to the ocean and then continue his voyage northward again in accordance with the instruction of Cortés. He, however, could discover no passage and, after several weeks' sailing, arrived at Santa Cruz, where he had been before. From there, after some detention, he resumed his voyage, still sailing south till he came to Cape San Lucas, the southern point of Lower California. This he doubled, and then ran up along the coast against cold northwesterly winds, keeping in sight of land all the way, until he came, on January 20, 1540, to a considerable island, now known as Cerros, which he called Cedros. There he landed and supplied his vessels with wood and water, after which he made several attempts to proceed further north. But each time he was driven back

by the northwest winds, which grew more and more violent
and compelled him to remain at the island until April.

By that time, many of his companions had become dissatisfied and insisted upon turning back. After some contro-
versy, Ulloa finally consented that the larger of his ships
might return; but, being determined to do his full duty, he
courageously and manfully picked out the boldest and brav-
est of the sailors; placed them in the smaller vessel, and with

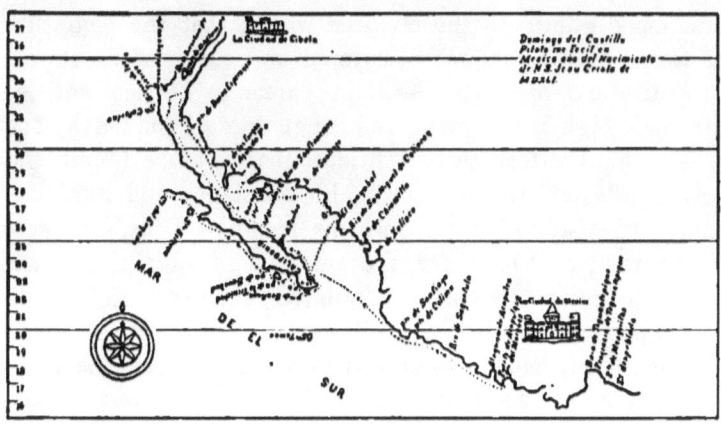

CASTILLO'S MAP OF LOWER CALIFORNIA.

[Showing Cabo Del Engaño and Ulloa's Route. From Venegas' "Noticia de la
California," etc. The inscription on the map, half Latin and half Spanish, reads
in English, "Domingo del Castillo, Pilot, made me in Mexico, in the year of the
birth of our Lord Jesus Christ, 1541."]

them, while the other ship turned southward before the
wind, he again beat up against the northwesterly gales. But
it seemed to be impossible for him to advance beyond a
point, about thirty leagues north of Cerros island, which he
called Cabo del Engaño—the Cape of Deceit. By that time
he found that his provisions would not last much longer, and
he was compelled to abandon the further prosecution of his
voyage northward. He accordingly turned south and fol-

lowed the other vessel as far as the coast of Jalisco, where he was basely assassinated by one of his own people.

With this voyage ended Cortés' connection with California. He failed to reach the best part of it or find any of its wealth. But he performed great and valuable services in its behalf. It was under his auspices that ships first breasted the waters of the North Pacific; that the west coast of Mexico was minutely examined; that the gulf of California, which in his honor was long known as the sea of Cortés, was first made known to the civilized world; that the peninsula of Lower California was discovered and surveyed in almost its entire extent. His brilliant career in Mexico entitles him to a high rank among the conquerors of the earth; but it is in his Californian expeditions that is to be found the best exhibition of his courage, his constancy and his fortitude. In 1540, after learning the result of Ulloa's voyage, he returned to Spain for the purpose of obtaining some acknowledgment for the six hundred thousand dollars he had expended in recent expeditions. It seems to have been his intention, had he succeeded in Spain, to come back to America and resume his search in the northwest. But, though received, as before, with shows of honor, he was obliged to spend the remaining seven years of his life in vain solicitations. His great spirit fretted against his enforced inactivity, and he died, still unheard and unrequited, at a little village near Seville in December, 1547.

SUGGESTIVE CORRELATIONS.

FOR THE PUPIL,

(To be studied with the Teacher.)

1. From what place did the expedition led by Narvaez start? How was he equipped? At what point in Florida did he land? How did he become separated from his ships?

How did he pursue his journey? Where and how did he lose his life? Where were a few of his men thrown ashore? From what point did they start on their wanderings? What do you remember about Narvaez and Cortés?

NOTE.—From the text you see how the experience of Cabeza de Vaca served to stimulate in the west the desire to explore the interior of the continent. It had the same effect in the east.

2. Who was authorized to conquer and occupy the country embraced within the patent of Narvaez? From what place did the expedition set out? When? How was it equipped? Where did it land? Trace briefly its wanderings. Did he find any kingdoms worth plundering? What was the principal event of the expedition? What was the fate of its leader? In what famous conquest had he taken part?

3. In what way did expeditions into the interior of the continent tend to correct the views commonly held as to a northwest passage?

TO THE PUPIL.

The following detached statements continue the story of The Conquest of Mexico. They trace the career of Cortés from the commencement of his march upon Mexico until he captured the city. Combine them as you did the previous ones into sentences and the sentences into paragraphs. The paragraphs that you can form are indicated in the grouping of the statements.

1. When Cortés began his march to Mexico, his force consisted of 450 Spaniards. Many of them were clad in mail. He had half-a-dozen small cannon. He had fifteen horses. The horses terrified the natives.

2. At one place the Spaniards were received as gods. A fierce tribe, known as the Tlascalans, did not believe this and offered battle. The Spaniards defeated them. The Tlascalans then made an alliance with the Spaniards. They did this because the Aztecs were their enemies. The allies then

marched towards Mexico. The chief of one town attempted to entrap the Spaniards. He did not succeed in doing so.

3. The Spaniards first saw the City of Mexico, November 7, 1519. They entered it next day. When Cortés had been in the city six days, he seized Montezuma. An attempt was made to release him by his brother and two chiefs. Cortés captured them and put them in irons. The people did not know what to do while Montezuma was alive and in captivity.

4. The long winter passed in quiet. In April, Cortés heard that Panfilo de Narvaez had anchored on the coast with eighteen ships and not less than twelve hundred men. He had been sent by Velasquez with orders to arrest Cortés. Cortés took three hundred men and marched at once to the Coast. He left one hundred and fifty men under Pedro de Alvarado to guard Montezuma and Mexico. He surprised, defeated and captured Narvaez. He enlisted the men in his service. He then marched back to Mexico. He arrived there the 24th of June. He saw at once that something terrible had happened while he had been away.

5. The Spaniards, left there, had massacred about six hundred of the people on the day of their spring festival. They had done so because they feared an attack. Many chiefs of clans were massacred.

6. As food was needed, Cortés released Montezuma's brother to open the markets. Instead of doing so, he called together the tribal council. It deposed Montezuma and elected him in his place. The Spaniards were fiercely attacked next morning. Montezuma tried to stop the attack. He could not. The people considered his authority gone. He was struck by a stone. He died on the last day of June. On the evening of the next day Cortés evacuated the city. The Indians fell upon his force in great numbers. It was a terrible night for him. It is known in history as "La Noche Triste—The Melancholy Night." Cortés wept. He did not for one moment, however, give up his purpose of taking Mexico.

7. In a few days the Indians attacked him in almost overwhelming force. He defeated them. He sent to Hispaniola for horses, cannon and soldiers. On April 28, 1521, he began the siege of Mexico. The fighting was incessant and terrible. At last, on the 13th of August, the city was captured.

CHAPTER IV.

CORONADO AND ALARCON.

ANTONIO DE MENDOZA, VICEROY.

[From "Los Gobernantes de Mexico."]

In the meanwhile Antonio de Mendoza, the viceroy of New Spain, set on foot two separate armaments for the conquest of Cíbola, one to go by land and the other by sea. The first was placed under command of Francisco Vasquez de Coronado, governor of Jalisco, who was ordered to follow the same course taken by Father Marcos de Niza. The second one was embarked upon ships and confided to Hernando de Alarcon, with instructions to sail along the coast as far as the latitude of Cíbola and then co-operate with the land army in subjugating the country. Coronado marched from Culiacan on April 22, 1540, with one hundred and fifty horsemen and two hundred infantry, besides some light pieces of artillery. He proceeded in a nearly northerly direction over a bare and rough region, passing several small streams and crossing a number of barren mountains and dry arid plains,

(15)

until in about a month he arrived at the far-famed seven cities. His imagination, as well as that of all his companions had been raised to the highest pitch of enthusiasm by the account of what Father Marcos de Niza had seen from the mountain; but all they could find, upon actually reaching the place, were several small towns, consisting indeed of large houses, with flat roofs, but without splendor or beauty, and inhabited by only a few hundred people. The country, however, was pleasant and the climate delightful. The soil in the neighborhood, though generally sandy, was in places fruitful and bore Indian corn, beans and pumpkins in great abundance. The natives were clothed, some in well-dressed skins and some in cotton garments. But there was little or no civilization, and neither gold, nor silver, nor turquoise, nor precious stones of any kind were to be seen.

Disappointed thus in not finding what he sought, Coronado proceeded northeastwardly and, traveling a week or two longer and passing a number of other towns of the same general character as those he had left, reached a large river, which flowed towards the gulf of Mexico. It was in fact what is now known as the Rio Grande. The plains along this river were covered with buffaloes in such immense herds as to be absolutely innumerable. In that neighborhood he heard of a rich country still further north, which was called Quivira and said to be governed by a king named Tatarrax, who wore a long beard, adored a golden cross and worshiped an image of the queen of heaven. It is not at all likely that Coronado, after what he had experienced, believed this story. But still it excited his curiosity and induced him to search it out. Accordingly, taking along thirty horsemen and leaving the main body of his army where he then was, he set out for the far north. He traveled continuously for thirty days more, and during all the time was constantly surrounded by bands of buffaloes. At length he reached Quivira, which seems to have been situated in the neighborhood of the Arkansas river and not far from the middle of the present state of Kansas. But though it exceeded Cíbola in the fame of its magnitude and wealth, it now on examination proved quite as poor and inconsiderable; and there was nothing to indicate any king or golden cross or image of the queen of heaven in the whole country.

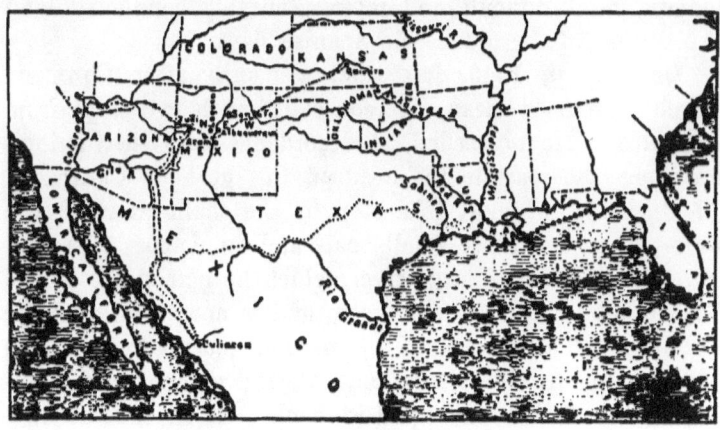

MAP INDICATING PIONEER ROUTES.

Cabeza de Vaca	....	Coronado	⌐-ı-ı-ı-ı-ı-ı-
Marcos de Niza	- - - - - - - -	Alarcon	ı-ı-ı-ı-ı-ı-ı-ı

By the time he had examined the neighborhood in different directions, the season was considerably advanced and Coronado resolved to hasten back. He therefore hurriedly set up a cross and inscription, commemorating his progress, and then, as rapidly as possible, retraced his steps to where he had left his main army. A few of his people, however, including Father Juan de Padilla, Father Luis de Escalona and a negro priest, had become so fascinated with the beautiful diversity of rolling hills, plains and streams at Quivira that they determined to remain. Unfortunately they kept with them a horse, a few mules, sheep and poultry and some ornaments, which so tempted the cupidity of the Quivirans that they soon afterwards despoiled and killed them all, except one, a Portuguese, who managed to escape and carry the melancholy intelligence of the massacre to the Spanish settlements. Coronado meanwhile, having rejoined his army, wintered on the Rio Grande river and the next year returned to New Spain. His march was one of the longest, most difficult and most admirably conducted land expeditions of the old heroic Spanish days.

On May 9, 1540, less than a month after Coronado marched from Culiacan, Alarcon sailed with two ships from Acapulco. He proceeded, in accordance with instructions, up along the coast to the head of the gulf of California. There, being brought to a stop by the shallowness of the water, he manned two small boats and on August 26 rowed into the mouth of a large river, which he named the Buena Guia but which has since been, and is now, known as the Colorado. This he ascended, in some places dragging his boats up against the strong current, and entered into intercourse with the Indians upon its banks. After thus advancing a considerable distance, he learned that Cíbola was thirty days' journey to the eastward of where he was, and that Coronado and his army were then there. He immediately tried to find means to communicate with them; but no one was willing to undertake the long and dangerous journey across the country. He thereupon returned to his ships and brought up all his small boats and as many of his men as they could carry, intending to march them in a body and effect the desired junction. But after many endeavors, finding that he could not hear anything further of Coronado, he at length gave up the attempt; and, a second time dropping down the river, he re-embarked in his vessels and returned to Acapulco. To him is due the discovery and

part navigation of the Colorado river. He is also entitled
to the praise of having distributed among the natives various
European seeds and poultry. But so little did the results of
his voyage satisfy the exorbitant expectations of the viceroy
Mendoza that, upon his return, he found himself disgraced
or at least neglected; and this unworthy treatment so wor-
ried and preyed upon his
spirits that he soon afterwards died.

PEDRO DE ALVARADO.
[From "Das Alte Mexiko."]

About the time of
Alarcon's return, and
while Coronado was still
absent at Cíbola and Qui-
vira, Pedro de Alvarado
collected a great fleet at
Navidad. He had twelve
ships and several smaller
vessels, well furnished
with provisions. He had
entered into a compact
with Mendoza, by the
terms of which all new
discoveries and conquests
were to be at their joint
expense and for their

mutual benefit. The two visited the fleet together and made
arrangements that everything should be in readiness to sail
in the spring of 1541. But it happened, as the appointed
time approached, that an insurrection broke out among the
Indians in the upper part of Jalisco; and, it being important
that the province which was to constitute the base of their
operations should be secure, Alvarado marched a portion of
his forces into the rebellious region. While conducting an
attack upon a rocky eminence where the insurgents had

fortified themselves, he was struck by an immense stone rolled down the declivity, thrown from his horse and so severely bruised that he died in four days afterwards.   By his death the fleet, which remained at Navidad, lost its leader; and, there being no one to take his place, the recruits disbanded and the ships lay idle at their moorings.   Nor was it until the next year that these vessels were put to any use, when Mendoza, after quelling the disturbance in Jalisco, took charge of them.   He, besides sending five across the Pacific to the Philippine islands, dispatched two under command of a Portuguese navigator of great reputation, named Juan Rodriguez Cabrillo, to California, with specific instructions to continue the examination of its outward 'coast beyond what had already been ascertained.

What was known of California at that time was delineated on an admirable map of the peninsula, with the gulf on one side and the ocean on the other as far north as Cabo del Engaño.   This map had been drawn in 1541 by Domingo del Castillo, the chief pilot of Alarcon's expedition.   He had evidently had access to the charts of Ulloa, for he not only gave the names of many places imposed by that navigator, but also outlined the coasts that had up to that time been visited by no one else.   In the shape and size of the peninsula, in the position of its headlands, bays and neighboring islands, and in the relative distances of noticeable points, he was surprisingly accurate.   And this is all the more remarkable, when taken in connection with the fact that, for many years afterwards, the new maps that were made were not nearly so correct.   Almost all of them for a century and upwards persisted in representing California as an island and for more than two centuries gave it a much distorted form.

SUGGESTIVE CORRELATIONS.

It is suggested that the pupil be not required at this time to remember the names of any Indian tribes, except those that they will name in answer to the fifth question. If later in the study of the "History of the United States," any tribe becomes of historical interest, attention can be called to the stock or race to which it belongs. In this way the pupil will ultimately not only know the principal stocks or races, but the important tribes that belong to each, without having made any special effort to do so.

FOR THE PUPIL.

(To be studied with the Teacher.)

If you have any difficulty in answering the questions below, refer to Chapter I, Fiske's "History of the United States."

1. Name the three principal groups of Indians as they existed in North and South America in 1492.
2. Name one of the tribes representing the division living to the west of Hudson's Bay and southwardly between the Rocky Mountains and the Pacific Coast as far as the northern parts of Mexico.
3. Name the three stocks or races living east of the Rocky Mountains.
4. Where was the home of the remaining division?
5. Name two tribes of this division that are of most interest to us, and tell where they live.
6. Of the three principal groups of Indians referred to in the first question, which wove excellent baskets? Which made pottery, or ornamental pipes or, in case of some tribes, coarse cloth? Fine cotton and woolen cloths were made by a tribe of which group? Which group had dogs? Which group had the llama and alpaca? Which lived in wigwams? Which in villages, with houses fitted to last some years and large enough to hold from thirty to fifty families? Which in pueblos? What two meanings has the word Pueblo?

7. Compare the three groups as to their progress in agriculture, government, religion, or in any important particulars.

8. In a short paragraph, tell what you can of the ancient Indians east of the Rocky Mountains.

REFERENCES.

A translation from the narrative of Juan Jaramillo, who has left the best itinerary of the expedition of Coronado, is selection No. 24—"First Expedition to Kansas and Nebraska"—in Hart's "American History told by Contemporaries," Vol. I. It is republished from the "Fourteenth Annual Report" of the Bureau of Ethnology. It is recommended that the pupils read the selection, or that the teacher read it to them, making running comment upon it.

McMaster's "School History of the United States."

"A New History of the United States," Scudder.

CHAPTER V.

CABRILLO.

JUAN RODRIGUEZ CABRILLO.
[From Art Collection in Golden Gate Park, San Francisco.]

Juan Rodriguez Cabrillo sailed from Navidad on June 27, 1542. His two ships were named respectively the San Salvador and the Victoria. On July 2 he reached Santa Cruz in Lower California. Passing thence around Cape San Lucas, he ran northwesterly along the coast, carefully examining it all the way, till on August 20 he arrived at Cabo del Engaño, now called Cabo Bajo, the most northerly point on that coast reached by Ulloa or known to the Spaniards. From that place he sailed into untraversed waters. The first place he stopped at was what is now known as Las Virgines, where he anchored and went through the form of taking possession of the country; and he did the same at the bay of Todos los Santos. Leaving this place, he passed the Coronados islands and at the end of September, 1542, entered the port of San Diego, called by

(21)

him San Miguel, and thus became the discoverer of Alta
California and the first white man that laid his eyes or placed
his feet upon its soil.

After a short stay at San Diego, Cabrillo sailed on and
discovered and visited the islands of San Clemente and
Santa Catalina. Turning thence to the mainland, he
anchored opposite an Indian town on the coast, where the
natives came out to his ships in numerous canoes, for which
reason he called the place Pueblo de las Canoas; and there
again he went through the formalities of taking possession
of the country. This place seems to have been at or near
what is now known as San Juan Capistrano. Pursuing his
voyage northwestwardly, he discovered the islands of Santa
Cruz, Santa Rosa and San Miguel, and, sailing up the channel between them and the mainland, found the coast along
there to be charming and populous. At one place, opposite
a beautiful valley, he anchored and traded with the natives,
who came out in their canoes with fresh fish. But when he
reached the long, low projection of Point Concepcion, the
northwesterly winds blew so violently that he deemed it prudent to run out to sea; and for a number of days he beat off
and on, without being able to make head against them. In
the meanwhile the temperature fell; the weather became
dark and lowering, and the storm increased to such a degree
that he was compelled to run back some forty leagues and
take shelter in a little port named Sardinas, in what was
called by the natives the province of Sejo. It appears to
have been at or not far from the present Santa Barbara.
While there he was visited by an aged Indian woman, said
to be the lady of the land, who remained for several days on
board his ship. She was attended by many of her people;
and it appears they all danced there to the sound of the
Spanish pipe and tambour.

From Sardinas, after replenishing his stock of wood and

water, and the weather meanwhile moderating, Cabrillo
again sailed to Point Concepcion, which he doubled, and
thence proceeded along the coast northwestwardly. It was
in general rough and rock-bound. On November 17 he
reached and doubled a prominent and well-wooded point,
then named and still called Point Pinos, and ran into what
was afterwards called Monterey Bay. There he anchored
and attempted to land, with the object of taking possession,

POINT OF PINES.

[From Sketch, made by W. B. McMurtrie in 1851, five miles S. ¾ W. (by
compass) from Point. Published in U. S. Coast Survey Chart of Monterey Harbor,
1852.]

but was prevented by the violence of the sea. Again proceeding still further northwest along a rugged coast with
high mountains, whose summits happened to be covered
with snow, he reached Point Año Nuevo, which he called
Nieve. He was now, had he only known it, almost within
sight of the grandest harbor in the world; but, the weather
continuing stormy and the prospect gloomy, he turned
around and ran down to the most westerly of the Santa Barbara islands, now known as San Miguel though named by
him Posesion, where he disembarked and determined to winter. And there, on January 3, 1543, he died, leaving Bartolomé Ferrelo, his chief pilot, in command of the expedition, with strict injunctions to continue his discoveries and
examine the entire coast as far as it was possible to follow it.

Ferrelo, having buried his dead commander on the island and given it the name of Juan Rodriguez in commemoration of the sad event, set sail for the mainland; but, finding the northwesterly winds still violent, he was compelled to return, and remained there until the middle of February. He then sailed for Sardinas, but found that all the Indians, apparently on account of the advance of the season, had disappeared from the coast. The sea also continued rough, making the anchorage unsafe; so that he deemed it prudent to turn about and run down to the island of San Clemente, which offered a better shelter against the rigor of the storm. After a short stay at that place, he ran out in a southwesterly direction in search of other islands; but, the winds suddenly changing and blowing strong from the southward, he determined to take advantage of them and sailed northwestward.

On February 25, he came again in sight of Point Pinos, which, however, he passed without stopping. He was carried along with such speed that on February 28 he discovered a very prominent point, which, in honor of the viceroy Mendoza, he called Cape Mendocino, the name which it still bears. There, the winds increasing to a violent gale, Ferrelo experienced such tumultuous blasts and heavy seas that the waves dashed over the ships; and, without being able to land or find shelter, he was driven to the northward in great risk and fear of being wrecked. There were signs of the coast not far off; but the fog was so thick that he could not see, except a very short distance before him. On March 1, the fog partially lifted, and he discovered Cape Blanco in the southern part of what is now Oregon. By this time, finding his provisions nearly gone and what were left more or less damaged, he felt compelled to turn again and ran southeasterly for San Clemente, where he intended to make another stay. But upon approaching that island in the night, the Victoria suddenly disappeared. Ferrelo, believing it lost yet deeming it his duty, without stopping, to make immediate search for it, sailed at once for the mainland and then down to San Diego, to Todos los Santos, to Las Virgines, and to Cerros island, where he arrived on March 24 and happily found the Victoria ahead of him. That little vessel, as it now appeared, had run over the rocks into the port of San Clemente on the night of separation and afterwards, not being able to find the San Salvador, had pursued its voyage alone as far as Cerros. From this place the two ships departed on April 2, sorely in want of provisions, and on April 18, after an absence of nearly a year, safely re-entered the port of Navidad.

Thus to Cabrillo belongs the honor of the discovery of Alta California and to him, in connection with his pilot Ferrelo, the credit of sailing along its entire coast and ascertaining its general shape and character. The nature of his expedition; the inadequacy of his little vessels, the smaller of them not even having a deck; the rigid season in which he executed his voyage; the fortitude displayed and the success attained—all stamp him as a daring and intrepid, as well as a careful and prudent, navigator. His death in the midst of his undertaking imparts a melancholy interest to his memory; and the touching solicitude for the prosecution of his enterprise, exhibited in his dying injunctions to Ferrelo, justifies posterity in rendering the tribute of admiration to the heroic sense of duty which must have animated him.

SUGGESTIVE CORRELATIONS.

TO THE PUPIL.

1. Make a list of the places on the coast of California at which Cabrillo or his chief pilot touched. Locate them on the map of California contained in your geography.

CHAPTER VI.

THE PHILIPPINE TRADE.

The information acquired by Cabrillo dissipated any hopes, that may have remained in the minds of the Spaniards, of finding India or even a second Mexico or Peru on the northwest coast. No indications of wealth could be seen; the miserable natives wore no ornaments of gold or silver or precious stones, and there were no exhibitions in the remotest degree pointing to rich kingdoms to be searched out or barbaric splendor to be won. Though the adventurers, in beating up along the sea-board, noticed the beauty of the country where they could see inland and caught glimpses here and there of some of its delightful valleys, and though they could not have failed to observe, notwithstanding the winds to which they were sometimes exposed, the general equability of the temperature and the glories of the climate, they could not appreciate such advantages, because these were not what they sought. The country was remote; and, as it promised nothing to tempt the cupidity or satisfy the avarice of the Spaniards, no further attention, perhaps, would have been paid to California, had it not been for other interests springing up in an entirely different section of the globe, thousands of miles away.

The interests referred to were those of the commerce growing out of the opening of a western passage from Spain to the spice islands of the East Indies and the establishment of the Spanish supremacy in the neighboring Philippines. The Portuguese had already taken possession of Ternate and

Tidore, having reached them by the way of the Cape of Good Hope, when Magellan, in the course of his navigation across the Pacific, discovered the Islas de Poniente or Islands of the Setting Sun, afterwards called the Philippines, which he claimed in the name and for the benefit of the Spanish crown. Here at last was not only accomplished the sublime idea, originally conceived by Columbus and always deemed of paramount importance by the Spanish court, of reaching Asia by sailing to the west; but here was also afforded to the Spaniards an opportunity of effecting a lodgment in, and maintaining a claim to, the famous and much-sought East Indies. Nor were they backward in taking advantage of it. Hardly had Magellan's discovery been announced, when several fleets were sent to follow his course and prosecute the Spanish claims in that quarter. In these objects all Spaniards took an interest, and for these purposes they were lavish of their treasure and their blood.

After many expeditions had been despatched, immense sums of money expended, and great numbers of lives lost, Miguel Lopez de Legaspi succeeded in 1565 in establishing the Spanish supremacy and imposing the Spanish sway upon the Philippine islands. And no sooner had this result been effected, than that extensive trade across the Pacific by means of Spanish galleons began, which continued for over two hundred years; enriched the Spanish treasury, and materially aided in making the Spanish nation for a time the wealthiest and most powerful in the world. In 1566 a galleon, called the San Gerónimo, the pioneer in this business, was sent out from Mexico; and the next year one of Legaspi's vessels returned thither. The navigation, thus commenced, soon ceased to be regarded as extraordinary and in a few years, as the winds and currents of the Pacific became better known, communication became frequent and regular. The annual galleons out from Mexico carried men, arms, unscrupulousness, chicanery and administrative ability; returning, they brought spices, silks, oriental treasures, jewels and gems.

Why was there a struggle between the Portuguese and the Spaniards in reference to the East Indies? And why did the Philippine trade take the way of America, instead of the Indian Ocean and the Cape of Good Hope? The answer to these questions is a curious and interesting one. It was on account of the respect paid by both nations to the authority of the pope. The Portuguese, when about initiating their voyages of discovery along the coast of Africa in search of a way to the Orient had solicited and obtained from the Roman pontiff a grant, so far at least as he could make one, of all the countries that should be discovered in t h e ocean as far as India,

SPANISH GALLEON.

[From " Les Marins du XV. et du XVI. Siècles."]

inclusive. Afterwards, when Columbus by sailing west discovered those islands of America, which he and all the world supposed to be a part of India, and took possession of them for the crown of Castile, a contest as to their title immediately arose between the Portuguese and Spaniards; and the result was a reference to the power, upon whose donation the Portuguese founded their claims. Alexander VI., then occupying the papal chair, unwilling to offend either party and apparently deeming the world wide .

enough for both, divided it between them and drew the famous line of demarcation north and south one hundred leagues west of the Cape de Verde and Azores islands, giving the Portuguese all east and the Spaniards all west of it. This line was afterwards, in 1494, at the instance of the Portuguese, fixed by treaty two hundred and seventy leagues further west.

So far all went well. The Portuguese pursued their dis-coveries towards the east and took possession of everything they could master in that direction; while the Spaniards did the same towards the west. But they met in the East Indian archipelago; and there the old strife was renewed. When Magellan discovered the Philippines, the Portuguese claimed them to be within their half of the world, while the Spaniards insisted to the contrary. Charts and maps were produced and longitudes calculated; but it was found that, to arrive at anything like a settlement of the line in that part of the world, it was necessary to ascertain the precise position of the line in the Atlantic, from which the count was to be made. Here a new difficulty presented itself. The Portuguese claimed it was three hundred and seventy leagues west of the most easterly of the Cape de Verde islands; the Spaniards that it was to be calculated from the most westerly. But, instead of resorting to the pope on this occasion, both nations agreed to refer the dispute to a convention of Spanish and Portuguese lawyers and cosmog-raphers, who met at Badajoz on the borders of Spain and Portugal in 1524. The result, as might have been antici-pated, was a disagreement. The Spanish judges decided in favor of Spain; and the Portuguese protested—thus leaving the question of title in the East Indies, as between the two nations, a fruitful source of long and bitter contention.

In addition to the rights of discovery east and west thus insisted upon, the same two nations also claimed the rights of exclusive navigation—the Portuguese of the route eastward around Africa, and the Spaniards of that westward by the way of America. Each, asserting such monstrous claims, felt itself obliged to pay a certain sort of respect to those of the other. And thus it was that not only the title of Spain to her American and East Indian provinces rested upon the assumed power of Pope Alexander VI. to give them

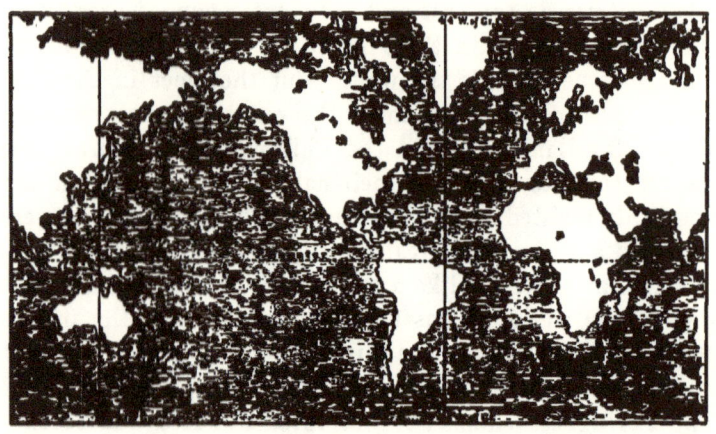

MAP ILLUSTRATING LINE OF DEMARCATION.

away; but it followed, as a consequence from such assumption and the division of the world in accordance with it, that the Spaniards were excluded from the Indian Ocean and the Cape of Good Hope, and their commerce with the East Indies was compelled to cross the Pacific.

What had all this to do with California? The answer is: a very great deal. It was soon found that the prevailing winds and currents of the ocean between America and Asia, while they favored a course within the tropics for vessels westward bound, rendered a much more northerly course almost a matter of necessity for their return. It was for this reason that the richly freighted galleons from the Philippines, upon leaving those islands, ran up beyond the tropics; then, taking advantage of the westerly winds and Japan current, crossed over to about Cape Mendocino, and from there ran down along the coast of California to Mexico and thence to Panama. The commerce so established produced three results very important to California. First, it attracted the attention of English privateers, who lost no favorable opportunity of depredating upon the Spanish colonies and trade. Secondly, it occasioned a renewal of the search for the straits, which were long supposed to connect the Atlantic and Pacific oceans to the north of America. And thirdly, it rendered the occupation and as far as practicable the defence of the Californian coast, along which the Philippine galleons were obliged to pass, a matter of very considerable concern.

SUGGESTIVE CORRELATIONS.

TO THE PUPIL.

1. In what way did the information acquired by Cabrillo dissipate the idea, that had been entertained by the Spaniards, that they were upon the threshold of India?
2. If it had not been for interests springing up in an entirely different part of the globe, would any further attention have been paid to California?
3. What interests are referred to?
4. What nation first reached India by an ocean route?
5. When, by whom, and in what direction, was the voyage made?
6. Were the Philippines east or west of the line of demarcation antipodal to the meridian 370° west of the Cape de Verde islands?

7. If the authority of the pope had been respected, as to the division of the world between the Portuguese and the Spanish, to which nation did the Moluccas belong? The Philippines?
8. To what nation do the Moluccas now belong? The Philippines? The island west of, and the archipelago to the southwest of, the Philippines?
9. Which of the Philippine islands is of the greatest importance? What city on its western coast?
10. Name five commercial products of the Philippines.
11. Is the fiber known as manila hemp true hemp fiber? Is it obtained from a tree or a plant? From what portion? How long is the fiber? What makes it cheap? From what plant is the fiber known as henequin or sisal hemp mainly derived? Why is it called sisal hemp? Have you ever seen a species of the plant from which this fiber is derived? What drink do the Mexicans make from a species of it? Locate Sisal in Yucatan, also Merida and Progresso. Which has the greater tenacity and endurance, a rope made of manila hemp or one of sisal? Which is the cheaper?
12. Why is a place where rope is made called a ropewalk? Have you ever read Longfellow's poem, "The Ropewalk"? If you have not, do so.

REFERENCES.

Chisholm's "Handbook of Commercial Geography," p. 138.
Romero's "Geographical and Statistical Notes on Mexico," p. 49.

FOR THE PUPIL.
(To be studied with the Teacher.)

The answers to the questions below are obtainable from Fiske's "The Discovery of America," Vol. II. The figures after the questions indicate the pages of the volumes where the answers can be found. After having carefully answered each question in a complete sentence, combine your sentences into a paragraph. The heading—The First Circumnavigation of the Earth—might be given to the paragraph.

1. Of what country was Magellan a native?—184.
2. When, with how many men and ships, from what po t, and in whose service, was he when he sailed on his voyage of circumnavigation of the globe?—191-192.
3. Give briefly the route of the voyage and some particulars of it. Include in your statement the first place touched after leaving port; the first place touched on the Brazilian coast; why the mouth of the La Plata was investigated; why he remained on the Patagonian coast from March 31 until August 24; what year it was; the date of the discovery of the Straits of Magellan; the course taken in the Pacific; and the first group of islands discovered.—193-204.
4. When did he reach the islands since named the Philippines?—209.
5. When, where and how did he lose his life?—205-206.
6. How many of his men and ships returned to tell the story of the first circumnavigation of the earth? When?—210.
7. As an achievement in ocean navigation, how does the voyage of Magellan compare with the first voyage of Columbus? Can you imagine anything that would surpass Magellan's voyage?—210.

REFERENCES.

A translation of the bull of Alexander VI. from the Latin into black-letter English is selection No. 18—"Papal Bull Dividing the New World"—in Hart's "American History told by Contemporaries," Vol. I. It is given in Latin and English, Appendix B, in Fiske's "The Discovery of America."

CHAPTER VII.

DRAKE AND NEW ALBION.

SIR FRANCIS DRAKE.

[From portrait by William Sharp, after Miraveldt, in Supervisors' Chamber, San Francisco.]

The first, the boldest and the ablest of the English adventurers, who preyed upon the Spanish commerce a n d settlements on the Pacific, was Francis Drake. He was born, within sight of the ocean, near Tavistock in Devonshire, and from very early years took to the sea. After several voyages across the Atlantic to the West Indies, in which he had many adventures and acquired a lasting hatred of t h e Spaniards, he resolved to fit out a privateering expedition and attack them in the Pacific. It was a project of the most daring character; but he evidently knew what he was about; and, when he got to work making his preparations, he found many prominent persons in England, even including Queen Elizabeth herself, to encourage and covertly contribute to his enterprise.

He sailed from Plymouth, England, on December 13, 1577, with five small vessels and one hundred and sixty-four

men. At Port St. Julien, on the eastern coast of Patagonia,
where he stopped for a while, he reduced the number of his
vessels to three, with which he sailed into the straits of
Magellan; and, after a long and tedious passage, in the
course of which both his attendant vessels separated from
him and returned home, he ran out into the Pacific. Contrary winds drove him southward for some distance; and he
discovered that the land south of Magellan's straits was an
island or group of islands, at the extremity of which the
Atlantic and Pacific oceans met; but, with constant attention and able seamanship, he at length succeeded in beating
up to northward and reached the Spanish settlements along
the coasts of Chile and Peru. He had now but a single vessel, of only one hundred tons burden, the name of which he
had changed from that of the Pelican to that of the Golden
Hind. But, notwithstanding this apparently inadequate
force, he resolutely attacked the Spaniards in various places;
seized and plundered several of their vessels between Valparaiso and Arica, and near Panama fought with and captured a richly laden ship, called the Cacafuego, from which
he took gold, silver, jewels and precious stones valued at
three hundred and sixty thousand dollars. From there, he
sailed up along the coast, taking several vessels carrying
spices, silks and velvets, and at one place landed and seized
still more gold, silver and jewels.

He then, being laden with spoil, began to think of
returning to England. In common with nearly everybody
else of his time, he believed in the existence of a passage to
the north of America; and he now resolved to seek it and
find his way through it into the Atlantic and thence back to
Plymouth. He accordingly ran far out into the ocean and
then turned towards the pole; but, after sailing for two
months and finding the weather growing rougher and rougher
and the seas more and more boisterous as he advanced, and his

heavily laden ship being ill-adapted for buffeting the constant head-winds, he thought proper to give up the search for the supposed straits and make for land, which he sighted near Cape Blanco in about latitude 43°, the furthest point northward reached by Ferrelo in 1543. From there, turning southward and running down the coast for a stopping place, he passed the long, projecting promontory of Point Reyes, on the south side of which he discovered "a

MAP OF DRAKE'S BAY.
[From Survey of the Rancho "Punta de los Reyes," approved by U. S. Surveyor-General, November 5, 1859.]

convenient and fit harbor," now known as Drake's bay; and there he came to anchor on June 17, 1579.

At this place he landed, set up a sort of fortification on the shore and remained thirty-six days. During that period, which it required to draw up his ship upon the beach and thoroughly clean, repair and refit it, he had several interviews with the natives. They were of very low grade, and seemed to take the English for superior beings. They approached with apparent reverence, bearing offerings of feather-ornaments, net-work, bows, arrows and quivers, skins of small animals, baskets of roots, seeds and other wild food, and little bags of what they called "tabah," probably something like wild tobacco. Drake, to disabuse their minds of the idea that the English were gods, caused religious services, according to the English episcopal ritual, to be performed in their presence, in which he and all his men knelt and joined in prayers, thus indicating that they were all but creatures of the one, only, Everlasting God. After prayers, psalms were sung; and with the music the Indians were especially delighted.

On the subsequent June 26, the natives, apparently from the entire region round about, collected in considerable numbers for the seeming purpose of doing honor to the strangers, and were marshaled by a tall, well-knit and finely-formed man, whom Drake supposed to be their chief or king. This person wore an exquisite head-dress and a mantle of squirrel or rabbit skins, which was thrown over his shoulders and hung down to his waist. He was accompanied, as is said, by a hundred warlike attendants. Before him marched a man bearing a stick of black wood four or five feet long, to which were attached two wreaths or crowns of net-work and feathers, three long strings of wampum or shell-work and a bag of tabah. This the English understood to be the royal mace or scepter. After him followed a multitude of men, entirely naked, with their long hair gathered at the back of the head and pinned with plumes or single feathers. All had their faces painted, some with white, some with black, some with other colors; and each bore a present. In the rear came the women and children, also bearing gifts. Upon getting near the camp, the scepter-bearer delivered an oration in a loud voice and then began a song and dance, in which the chief, or hioh as he was called, and all his attendants joined. Thus, singing and dancing, but with the utmost gravity, they approached the camp; and, after several turns around it, they addressed themselves to Drake at great length and in such a manner that he seems to have supposed they offered him their province, resigned their right and title to the country and made themselves and their posterity vassals to the English crown. They appear in fact to have placed a feather-crown upon his head, to have thrown about his neck their strings of wampum, saluted him with the name of "hioh," and then broken out into a song and dance of so loud and lively a character that it was deemed one of triumph.

The whole ceremony appears to have been nothing more than an expression of desire on the part of the Indians to make the English commander a chief amongst them, including his investiture with the honors and dignities of the station. The English could not understand their language, nor was it possible for the Indians to communicate the ideas of dominion or vassalage, which were beyond their experience or knowledge. On the other hand, the English in general knew nothing of the Indian tribal regulations; but, bringing with them only their experience of European institutions, they supposed the country to be a kingdom and the head-man of one of its numerous rancherias to be its king. Whatever Drake's own personal opinion as a man of broad observation and wide experience may have been as to the real meaning of their actions, he was not disposed to neglect so favorable an opportunity of construing them into a tender of the sovereignty of a vast territory, which might at some day be of value and importance to his native land; and accordingly he willingly accepted the supposed scepter, crown, and royal dignity and took formal possession of the country in the name of Queen Elizabeth for the use and benefit of the English nation.

Before re-embarking, Drake and a number of his company made a short excursion inland. They found the coun-

try there very different from the barren shore. Its green
slopes were covered with thousands of deer and almost
infinite numbers of small burrowing animals, probably
ground squirrels, but called by the English conies. The
weather also was much more pleasant than on the immediate
coast. The excursion being necessarily made on foot,
extended only a few miles. Some of the pine woods back
of Point Reyes, and perhaps some of the redwood forests,
and it may be some of the sheltered valleys, were seen.
But there were no wide or distant views; and so the English
under Drake, like the Spaniards under Cabrillo, though
within less than a day's travel of the most spacious and
magnificent bay in the world, had no idea of its existence.

Being now ready to sail, Drake set up, by way of memorial of his having been there and taken possession of the
country, a large post, firmly planted, upon which he caused
to be nailed a plate of brass, engraven with the name of the
English queen, the day and year of his arrival, the voluntary
submission of the country by both king and people to English sovereignty, and, underneath all, his own name. Fas-
tened to the plate was an English sixpence of recent coin-
age, so placed as to exhibit her majesty's likeness and arms.
At the same time, partly on account of the possession so
taken, but more especially because of "the white banks and
cliffs, which lie towards the sea," Drake named the country
New Albion—the word Albion meaning white and being also
sometimes used as a name of England. He supposed himself to be its discoverer and was not aware that thirty-six
years previous the Spaniards had passed along the same
coast and anticipated him.

On July 23, after many ceremonies of a religious character, singing of psalms and taking farewell of the sorrowing
natives, he stood out to sea. As his ship pursued its course
and lessened in the distance, the Indians ran to the tops of

their hills to keep it in view as long as possible and lighted fires, which indicated, long after they themselves could be distinguished from the vessel, that they were still watch-

PRAYER-BOOK CROSS.

[Erected in Golden Gate Park, San Francisco, in commemoration of Christian services at Drake's Bay in 1579.]

ful and were still doubtless turning their straining eyes and uplifted arms towards the departing strangers. The next morning, Drake found himself near the Farallones, called by him the islands of St. James, at one of which he stopped and killed seals and birds. He then ran directly for the East Indies, and from there sailed by the way of the Indian ocean and around the Cape of Good Hope to England, arriving at Plymouth with all his treasures on September 26, 1580, after an ab-

sence of nearly three years.   His great exploit, one of the most remarkable ever accomplished, rendered him famous throughout the civilized world. Four months after his return he was knighted and thus became Sir Francis Drake; and the queen, to do him special honor, dined on board his ship.

SUGGESTIVE CORRELATIONS.

TO THE PUPIL.

1. In what part of England is Plymouth?
2. Who sailed from that port for the Atlantic coast of America, September 16, 1620?

3. In what direction from Plymouth is Tavistock?
4. In what year did Queen Elizabeth ascend the English throne? How long did she reign?
5. In what respect does the motive that Drake had in making his voyage differ from that of Cabrillo?
6. Of what was he in search when he reached Cape Blanco?
7. How many years after the discovery of Drake's Bay was the battle of Bunker Hill fought?
8. In what direction from the Golden Gate are the Farallones?
9. Of what county are they a part?
10. What use is made of them by the United States Government?

MEMORIZE.

Sir Francis Drake made the second circumnavigation of the globe, 1577-1580.

He discovered Drake's Bay, June 17, 1579.

He held the first Christian service in the English tongue on our coast.

REFERENCES.

In connection with this chapter you should read selection No. 30—"The Famous Voyage of Sir Francis Drake about the Whole Globe," also No. 31—"The Piety of a Sea Rover," in Hart's "American History told by Contemporaries," Vol. I.

1. Of what advantage will it be to you to read these documents?
2. Why are such sources of value to historians?

SUBJECTS FOR ORAL DISCUSSION OR WRITTEN EXERCISES.

The effect of Drake's voyage upon the geographical knowledge of North America.

A description of Drake's Bay.

The Prayer Book Cross in Golden Gate Park.

1. In commemoration of what?
2. Why placed in Golden Gate Park instead of at Drake's Bay?
3. Its location, the view from it, etc.
4. The material of its construction.
5. Something of the man who presented it.

NOTE.—The inscription upon the cross is as follows:

"Presented to Golden Gate Park at the opening of the Midwinter Fair, January 1, A. D. 1894, as a memorial of the service held on the shore of Drake's Bay about Saint John Baptist's Day, June 24, Anno Domini 1579, by Francis Fletcher, priest of the Church of England, chaplain of Sir Francis Drake, chronicler of the service. Gift of George W. Childs, Esquire, of Philadelphia.

"First Christian service in the English tongue on our coast. First use of the Book of Common Prayer in our country. One of the first recorded missionary prayers on our continent. Soli Deo sit semper gloria."

The last sentence of the above inscription is in Latin, and means "To the only God, let there be glory forever."

If there is some place of historic interest in the State, in which you are particularly interested, but which you can not visit, write to the Superintendent of Public Schools of the County in which it is situated, and ask him to give you the names of some school children, who would write you about it. You should also offer to describe something in your neighborhood, in which they might be interested but could not visit.

CHAPTER VIII.

CAVENDISH, WOODES ROGERS, AND SHELVOCKE.

SIR THOMAS CAVENDISH.

[From "Lives and Voyages of Drake, Cavendish, and Dampier," etc., Harper & Bros., New York, 1873.]

The fame and particularly the wealth acquired by Drake induced an English gentleman, named Thomas Cavendish, to follow in his wake not long afterwards. He sailed from Plymouth on July 21, 1586, with three small vessels and one hundred and twenty-three men. Having passed the straits of Magellan and entered the Pacific by the end of February, he sailed up the west coast of South America, seized and destroyed several small Spanish ships, and landed at, plundered and burned the town of Payta in Peru. Proceeding thence to the westerly coast of Mexico, he landed at and burned Guatulco and destroyed several vessels in the shipyard of Navidad. On September 20, he was at Mazatlan, where he abandoned the smaller of his ships; and with the other two, the larger of which was only of one hundred and twenty

(39)

tons and the smaller only half so large, he sailed over to
Lower California to lie in wait for the annual galleon from
the Philippines. He arrived at Cape San Lucas on October
14 and remained till November 4, when the object of his
search hove in sight. Cavendish immediately gave chase
and, after a long run and a severe conflict, succeeded in cap-
turing it. The prize proved to be a vessel, called the Santa
Anna, of seven hundred tons burden, carrying one hundred
and ninety persons, mostly passengers, including a number
of women, and a cargo of two hundred and forty-four thousand dollars in gold, besides large quantities of satin, silk,
musk and other East Indian merchandise.

After securing their prisoners, the captors carried the
prize into a port, called Aguada Segura, on the easterly side
of Cape San Lucas, where they put the captives on shore,
transferred the gold and other most valuable portions of the
cargo to their own vessels, and then set the Santa Anna on
fire. As they did so, they fired a final gun as a parting
knell and sailed away with their plunder. Upon leaving
Cape San Lucas, Cavendish bore for the East Indies; but
scarcely had he lost sight of port, when a violent storm
arose, which separated his ships, and the smaller of them
was lost. Fortunately for the despoiled and despairing passengers on land, the same storm drove the burning prize
upon the beach and thus afforded them an unexpected means
of escaping their forlorn situation on a remote and desolate
coast. There happened to be among them a man, named
Sebastian Viscaino, who afterwards became a famous navigator in Californian waters. As he beheld the flaming hulk
driving in towards him, he at once organized the forces at
hand; ran out to meet the promised rescue; boarded the
fiery pile and, aided by the rain, soon extinguished the
flames. He found a sound hull and in a short time made
out of it a sufficiently safe conveyance to transport himself

and his companions across the gulf of California to the Spanish settlements on the other side, whence all finally reached their destination. Meanwhile Cavendish, with one vessel, kept on his way across the Pacific. In due time he reached the East Indies, whence he sailed to the Cape of Good Hope and on September 9, 1588, after an absence of two years and fifty days, arrived with his spoil at Plymouth. He too, like his predecessor, was knighted by the English queen, and was thereafter known as Sir Thomas Cavendish.

It was not for more than a hundred years after Drake and Cavendish, that the next great English privateersman appeared in the Pacific and visited California. This was Captain Woodes Rogers, who, no less than they, "filled with terror all the coasts of the South Sea." He sailed from Bristol with two ships and three hundred and thirty-three men on August 1, 1708. The larger vessel was of three hundred and twenty tons burden and carried thirty guns, the smaller of two hundred and sixty tons and twenty-six guns. They doubled Cape Horn about the beginning of 1709 and at the end of January reached the island of Juan Fernandez, which lies in the wide ocean four hundred miles west of Valparaiso in Chile. There they found and rescued the celebrated Alexander Selkirk, a Scotch sailor, who had been abandoned on the island four years and four months previously by the captain of an English vessel, named Stradling. He came on board of Rogers' ship clothed in goat skins, looking wilder than the animals whose coats he wore, and told the affecting story of his desolation, his melancholy, his griefs, his terrors; how he gradually came to recover his spirits; his shifts and contrivances; how by the life he was compelled to lead he was "cleared of all gross humors" and became as agile and active as the wild goats which he pursued; how he caught kids, tamed them to be his companions, taught them to dance with him and thus while away the

tedious hours of his solitude—in fine his narrative was the
original upon which Daniel Defoe founded his beautiful
and intensely interesting story of "Robinson Crusoe."

From Juan Fernandez Rogers sailed for the coast of
Peru, where he took and plundered a number of Spanish
vessels. As he advanced northward he seized the town of
Guayaquil in Ecuador and held it until ransomed. From
Guayaquil he sailed by way of the Gallapagos islands to the
coast of California and there cruised for the Philippine
galleon, which was expected about the end of the year. By
that time, more than a hundred years after Drake and Cavendish, during which the Spanish ships in the Pacific pursued their courses and carried their treasures undisturbed by
English privateers, the Philippine trade had increased so
much that the annual galleon or galleons, for there were
often more than one, carried treasure and merchandise sometimes amounting in value to ten millions of dollars. He
arrived at Cape San Lucas on November 1, 1709, and on
December 21, espied, chased, attacked and, after a desperate
conflict, captured a richly freighted Philippine galleon
called Nuestra Señora de la Incarnacion y Desengaño.

From his prisoners, he learned that a second galleon,
called the Bigonia, still more richly freighted, was not far
behind. This also he chased and attacked, but the Spaniards fought with great valor and finally succeeded in beating off the English. Their success was due principally to
the extraordinary spirit of the chief gunner, who compelled
his men to keep up the fight by stationing himself in the
powder-room and taking a solemn oath that he would blow
the ship and all on board into atoms rather than allow it to
fall into the hands of the assailants. After the escape of the
Bigonia, the English, who had lost thirty men killed and
wounded and had their rigging badly damaged, repaired
their vessels and then sailed, taking their prize along, by

way of the Ladrones, Java and the Cape of Good Hope, to England, where they arrived in October, 1711.

The only other English privateersman of note that touched on the coast of California, though various others sailed into the Pacific and depredated upon the Spaniards, was Captain George Shelvocke. He left Plymouth on February 13, 1719, in company with Captain John Clipperton, each in command of a ship; but they soon separated and each pursued an independent voyage. Shelvocke was far from having the resolute and commanding spirit of a Drake, the strong and determined energy of a Cavendish or the unremitting, indefatigable tact of a Rogers. On the contrary, he showed himself to be a bickerer and a blusterer; and his vessel appears to have been a scene of almost continual dissension and disobedience. Among others with whom he disputed and quarreled was his first officer or mate, a fellow of morose and gloomy disposition, named Simon Hatley, who had been with Woodes Rogers in the Pacific and presumed to know a great deal more about the conduct of the voyage than his superior. It was this same Hatley, and upon this same voyage, that shot the albatross, afterwards rendered famous by Coleridge in his "Rime of the Ancient Mariner." When the ship was attempting to double Cape Horn and was buffeting against continuous storms of rain and sleet, a solitary black albatross, which had apparently lost its way, hovered around and for many days accompanied the vessel in its struggles through those dreary and desolate seas. Hatley, either regarding the bird as a breeder of storm and portent of further ill-fortune, or more probably actuated by a spirit of wanton cruelty, shot the poor creature. But his hopes of more favorable winds, if he entertained any, were not realized; the blast continued to blow as fiercely and the waves to roll as tumultuously as before; and for a long time it seemed doubtful whether the ship would be able to weather the cape. However, after a rough and protracted run and suffering great hardships, which were rendered still more poignant by the state of feeling existing on shipboard, the adventurers finally succeeded in reaching the Pacific and meeting smoother waters.

Shelvocke committed ravages along the coast of Chile and Peru; plundered a number of small vessels, and set fire to the town of Payta; but his cruise was in nearly every respect ill-conducted, and he gained no spoil of much value. He lost the vessel in which he had sailed at the island of Juan Fernandez, but afterwards seized a substitute from the Spaniards, in which he continued his voyage. In 1721 he ran north of the equator and met Captain Clipperton, whom he had not seen for two years; and the two agreed to watch for the next Philippine galleon; but Clipperton soon grew dissatisfied and, without giving any notice, sailed for China. Shelvocke, finding himself deserted, committed some further depredations on the coast of Mexico and then ran to Cape San Lucas, where he arrived on August 11 and remained a week supplying his vessel with wood and water, after which he also sailed to China. There, by various fraudulent subterfuges as is said, he got rid of his ship and finally managed, though with considerable difficulty on account of the ill-feeling he provoked, to secure passage to London, where he arrived in August, 1722. The main spoils he carried were the proceeds of his ship. In England, he was arrested and prosecuted for piracy and fraud; but, on account of the difficulty of procuring evidence of what had taken place on the other side of the world and by disgorging, as is further said, a portion of his ill-gotten gains, he succeeded in escaping conviction and fled the kingdom.

SUGGESTIVE CORRELATIONS.

1. What motive had Cavendish, Rogers, and Shelvocke in making their voyages?
1. From what place did each sail?
3. Did either of them touch upon the coast of any part of the present State of California?
4. Who sailed in May, 1497, from the same port as Rogers, on a voyage of discovery?
5. Which of the English privateersmen is described as a "bickerer and a blusterer"? Which as having a "resolute and commanding spirit"? Which as having a "strong and determined energy"? Which as having an "unremitting, indefatigable tact"?
6. Make a list of the places on the coast of South America at which Drake, Cavendish, Rogers, or Shelvocke touched. Locate them on the map of South America contained in your geography.
7. Make a similar list of places at which they touched on the coast of New Spain. Locate them on the map facing page 6. See if you can find some of the same places on the map of Mexico contained in your geography.

FOR THE PUPIL.

(To be studied with the Teacher.)

1. In what latitude is the island of Juan Fernandez?
2. When, and by whom, was it discovered?
3. Who was the author of "Robinson Crusoe"?
4. When was he born?
5. When did he die?
6. When was "Robinson Crusoe" published?
7. Why has it "stimulated adventure and prompted young men to resort to the border lands of civilization"?
8. Where are the Gallapagos islands?
9. What is their latitude and longitude?
10. To what country do they belong?
11. What description did Charles Darwin make of the animal life found on the islands when he visited them on his voyage round the world in the ship Beagle?
12. From what do the islands derive their name?

REFERENCES.

"Crusoe's Island," by Frederick A. Ober, D. Appleton, New York, 1898, is nearly as interesting as "Robinson Crusoe." It is suggested that the teacher read the introduction by Dr. William T. Harris, United States Commissioner of Education, and that the attention of the pupils be called to the appendix.

"What Mr. Darwin Saw," etc. Harper & Bros., New York, 1880.

CHAPTER IX.

THE STRAITS OF ANIAN.

The Spanish commerce in the Pacific and more especially the Philippine trade not only attracted the English
privateers, as has been seen, but occasioned a renewal of the

MAP SHOWING SUPPOSED STRAITS OF ANIAN.

[From Zaltieri's Map of 1566, published in Venice and followed by Ortelin's
in 1570.]

search for the straits supposed to connect the Atlantic and
Pacific to the north of America. A passage of this kind,
called the "Straits of Anian," was reported to have been
found by Gaspar Cortereal, a Portuguese, who explored the
coasts of Labrador in 1499 and 1500; and from that time,
notwithstanding attempts to find it and repeated failures,
everybody believed in its existence. In the time of Cortés,

it was supposed to extend from Newfoundland on the one side to the East Indies on the other; and he even possessed a chart upon which it was so delineated. The report of Father Marcos de Niza of a sea near the Seven Cities of Cíbola was supposed to refer to the same passage; and it was the main object of Alarcon in 1540 to sail into it and thence communicate with Coronado. Cabrillo also in 1542 looked upon it as one of the objective points of his expedition; and it was doubtless in the hope and anticipation of its eventual discovery that, when he found himself stricken by the hand of death, he so earnestly adjured his second-in-command to prosecute and complete his voyage.

The first report of the actual finding of the passage was to the effect that Andres de Urdaneta had discovered it about 1556 and traced its course with great particularity upon a map, and that Martin Chaque had also discovered it about the same time. In 1574 Juan Fernandez de Ladrillero, an old pilot, who had navigated the Pacific for thirty-eight years, affirmed in a judicial trial in Spain the existence of the passage from one ocean to the other in about the parallel of Newfoundland. In 1582 Francisco Gali sailed from the Philippine islands much further to the northward than the track usually taken by the galleons, intending, by skirting the coast from China all the way round to Mexico, to ascertain whether it was continuous or not. Had he followed this course, he would have done great service and his name would have come down proudly in the first rank of discoverers. But he did not carry out his intentions. He merely found, in the course he took, a spacious extent of sea. But the waters were of great depth, with strong currents from the north and filled with whales and such kinds of fish as are said to frequent canals; and from these circumstances he affirmed the existence of, and expressed his belief in the straits, though he did not pretend to have seen them.

It was reserved for a Portuguese, named Lorenzo Ferrer de Maldonado, to put the finishing touch of fabrication upon the stories about the straits of Anian. He pretended to have sailed from Lisbon to Labrador in 1588 and thence by a direct passage into the Pacific and back again. According to his account, the navigation from Portugal to China by that route could be made in three months; and, not being chary of particulars, he gave every crook of his reported channel, with courses, distances, widths, currents and winds, and a minute description of the land on both sides. His fabrications do not appear to have imposed upon the world at the time; but they were revived some two hundred years afterwards by the finding of copies of his papers, and many persons, who ought to have known better, believed in them. Drake, in the course of his voyage across the Pacific, upon occasion of a quarrel with his chaplain, compelled the poor parson to wear a badge with the inscription, "Francis Fletcher, ye falseth knave that liveth." A badge and inscription of this kind would have been much more appropriate for Maldonado, unless, perhaps, he ought rather to be regarded as a man of unsettled mind, more an object of pity than reproach.

Next in celebrity of those, who pretended to have navigated and to give a particular description of the supposed straits, was a Greek pilot, named Apostolos Valerianus, but more commonly known as Juan de Fuca. He said of himself that he had followed the sea for nearly forty years in the service of Spain until the autumn of 1587 when, with Sebastian Viscaino, he was taken, by Cavendish, in the Philippine galleon Santa Anna off Cape San Lucas. He said he had been robbed on that occasion of goods worth sixty thousand ducats. He added that he had at once proceeded to Mexico; and that, it being then supposed that Drake and Cavendish had reached the Pacific by the straits of Anian, two sepa-

rate expeditions had been sent out from New Spain to re-
discover and fortify them and thus prevent any further
ingress, by that passage, of English privateers. He had been
pilot of the first of these expeditions, which failed on
account of mutiny; but in the second, which took place in
1592 under his own command, he had sailed up along
the coast of New Spain and California to latitude 47°
north, where he found an inlet thirty or forty leagues
wide, which he entered and navigated eastwardly for twenty
days. He said he had passed a number of islands, found
the natives clothed in the skins of wild beasts and the country fruitful and rich in gold, silver and pearls. He finally
reached the Atlantic Ocean; and then, having thus accomplished his mission, he turned round and returned to Mexico and claimed pay for his services, which, however, he
never received. Such was his story; and there was plainly
little, if any, more truth in it than in that of Maldonado;
but some two hundred years afterwards, when the subject of
the northwest coast was largely discussed on account of the
discovery of the great inlet leading into Puget Sound, which
was found to correspond in many respects with the old
pilot's account of the western end of his passage, the name of
Juan de Fuca was given to it and thus rescued from
oblivion.

In 1595, thirteen years after the voyage of Gali from the
Philippines, there appears to have been sent out from the
same islands by the governor, at the instance of the king of
Spain, a ship called the San Agustin. The object was to
examine the same coasts which it had been Gali's purpose to
skirt along and investigate. The vessel was intrusted to the
command of Sebastian Rodriguez Cermeñon. But where he
went and what he saw were never known, for the reason that
the ship with all on board was lost. It was afterwards reported to have reached what is now known as the bay of San

Francisco and to have been there driven on shore and broken to pieces. And it was also said that Viscaino in 1603 entered the same bay for the purpose of seeing whether he could not find the remnants of the old ship thus wrecked. But when it is considered that the present bay of San Francisco was not known until nearly two hundred years after the voyage of the San Agustin, and that Viscaino certainly never entered it for any purpose, it is plain that the reported wreck in that bay must be classed with the stories of Maldonado and De Fuca.

At the same time the facts, that such stories were concocted and told and that Gali and Cermeñon sailed, indicate that the belief in the straits of Anian continued to have a hold upon the public mind. And it became more and more plain to the Spaniards that, if this belief were well founded, their commerce in the Pacific would be exposed to great dangers. If the English and other enemies of Spain could find so short a way into the Pacific, it was obviously of the first importance to provide stations for the protection of ships engaged in trade, or, still better, to seize upon and fortify the passage itself. As there was, so far, no settlement of any kind along the entire coast of California, the importance of the occupation of that coast, as a preliminary to that of the supposed straits further north, became more and more apparent. It was under these circumstances that a new expedition, including an attempt to settle California, was determined on; and Sebastian Viscaino, the same man who had been taken prisoner by Cavendish at Cape San Lucas in 1587 and was so prompt and handy and successful in saving himself and his companions, was named leader of the expedition.

SUGGESTIVE CORRELATIONS.

TO THE TEACHER.

The idea of a northwest passage was one of the conse-quences of the voyage of Magellan. That voyage, with preced-ing ones, proved that the coast line of what we call America was continuous from the St. John's River in Florida to the Straits of Magellan.

The aim of the following questions is to show this to be the fact. They are not to be considered as exhaustive, but only suggestive. It is expected that additional ones will be asked, or that some will be omitted, as may be determined by the age and capabilities of the pupils, and whether the chapter is being studied for the first time or is being reviewed.

FOR THE PUPIL.

(To be studied with the Teacher.)

1. Who landed a little north of the site of St. Augustine in Florida on Easter Sunday, March 27, 1513? Of what was he in search; and in what direction, and how far, did he follow the coast line of that peninsula?
2. What portion of the coast of North America did Pinzon and Solis visit in 1498? Who was one of the pilots and chief cosmographers of the expedition? Why was the voyage not followed up, and why did it come to be nearly forgotten?
3. Who determined in 1519 that Florida was not an island by following the coast as far as Tampico, and, on returning, discovered the Mississippi river?
4. Why did this voyage increase the interest in the country to the northward? Why did Magellan's voyage?
5. Who was sent by the Spanish government to the Straits of Magellan in 1525? What discovery was made by one of the vessels, and why did it not attract general attention?
6. What did Drake determine about the land south of Magel-lan straits?
7. Did Magellan sail around the southern extremity of South America? Did Drake?
8. After whom was the southern extremity of South America named? Why?

TO THE TEACHER.

The aim of the following questions is to trace the search of the northwest passage on the Atlantic coast from the first attempt until the modern era of Arctic exploration.

FOR THE PUPIL.

(To be studied with the Teacher.)

1. When and by whom was the first attempt made to find a northwest passage? What river and bay did he try in the hope of finding a passage?

2. When and about where did the same man attempt to build a town? What did he call the place he built, and what was its fate?

3. Along what portion of the Atlantic coast did Estevan Gomez sail? What was the date of his voyage? What inlets did he notice?

4. Name the French navigator who preceded Gomez. When, and where, did he first sight land? In what direction did he skirt the coast? Give some particulars of his voyage.

5. Why did the search for the northwest passage become restricted to the Arctic regions?

6. What was the result of the search in Arctic waters by Sir Martin Frobisher? By John Davis?

7. Were any attempts made to find a northern passage around Siberia into the Pacific?

8. In whose service had Hudson been, before his voyage of 1609? How many voyages had he made previous to that date? What direction had he taken in his previous attempts? In whose service was he when he made his final voyage? What was his fate? Why did his attempts limit the search to the only really available route?

9. Who resumed the search in 1615?

10. Who opened the modern era of Arctic exploration?

REFERENCES.

A translation of the account of the voyage of the navigator referred to in the fourth question, written by himself, is contained in Hart's "American History told by Contemporaries," Vol. I. It is selection 34 and is entitled—"A Voyage Along the Atlantic Coast."

Fiske's "The Discovery of America," Vol. II. Chapter XII.

CHAPTER X.

VISCAINO.

SEBASTIAN VISCAINO.

[From Art Collection in Golden Gate Park, San Francisco.]

Viscaino sailed, with three ships, from Acapulco in the spring of 1596. He carried a number of soldiers and settlers, and also f o u r priests. He proceeded to Mazatlan and thence crossed to the place theretofore known a s Santa Cruz, where Cortés had attempted to make a settlement sixty years before. There he established a camp, built a stockade, erected a small church, put up a number of huts, and thus made a beginning of what was intended to be a permanent occupation. The place seemed so pleasant and the neighboring natives so peaceable that he called it La Paz—a name which it has ever since borne. But, on account of its rocks and small extent of cultivable ground, he soon recognized the fact that it was not suited for the purposes of a large colony; and he therefore despatched one

(50.)

of his vessels with a launch up the gulf to search for a more
favorable location. This ship proceeded up the coast a hundred leagues and landed a party of about sixty soldiers to
examine the country. Finding it no better than other
places, which they had passed, they commenced re-embarking, when they were attacked by the natives. A fight
occurred in which, though many of the Indians were killed,
nineteen of their own number lost their lives, some by
drowning and some by the hands of their assailants. On
account of this sad event and its failure to find what it
sought, besides scarcity of provisions, the ship turned round
and ran back to La Paz. Meanwhile the colonists there
had very nearly exhausted their stores; and, as there was no
possibility of obtaining supplies anywhere upon that coast,
Viscaino resolved to abandon the country and, re-embarking
with all his remaining people, returned to New Spain about
the end of the same year 1596.

Notwithstanding the ill-success of the last expedition,
the Spanish crown determined upon a new one in the same
direction. But this one was rather with the object of exploration along the coast of California than of actual settlement.
Reports of the existence of the straits of Anian were still rife;
and it was resolved, if possible, to find out the truth. By
order of the king, accordingly, a new outfit, consisting of
two large and two small vessels, was prepared by Gaspar de
Zuñiga, Conde de Monterey and viceroy of New Spain, and
placed under the charge of the same Sebastian Viscaino.
Upon this, which is known as his second voyage to California, Viscaino sailed from Acapulco on May 5, 1602. He
proceeded up the coast to the parallel of Cape San Lucas,
when he crossed the gulf and anchored in the bay known at
one time as Aguada Segura, at another as Puerto Seguro, by
him called San Bernarbé and now known as San José del
Cabo. From there he sailed on July 5 and carefully ex-

amined Magdalena bay, Cerros island and every other place
that seemed to offer promise of advantage for settlement; but
found none until he came to San Diego, where he arrived on
November 10 and remained ten days.   Some of his people
went up the promontory now known as Point Loma, which
separates the harbor from the ocean and shields it from the
northwest winds; and tak-
ing in a view of the entire
port, they pronounced it
one of the finest character
and very extensive.

COUNT OF MONTEREY, Viceroy.
[From " Los Gobernantes de Mexico."]

Thence Viscaino pro-
ceeded to the island, discovered by Cabrillo and
called by him Victoria but
by Viscaino, on account of
the day on which he ar-
rived there, given its present name of Santa Catalina.
He found many Indians
there, having large dwell-
ings and numerous ranch-
erias, with admirably con-
structed canoes, wearing
clothing of seal-skins and
being expert seal-hunters
and fishermen.   There were
many things of interest on the island; but the most extraordinary were a sort of temple, consisting of a large circular place
ornamented with variously colored feathers, and an idol in
the center supposed to represent the devil and having at its
sides representations of the sun and moon.   When the Spanish soldiers, who were conducted by an Indian, arrived at

the spot, they found two extraordinary crows, much larger than common, which, upon their approach, flew away and perched on neighboring rocks. Struck with their great size, the soldiers shot and killed both, whereupon their Indian guide began to utter the most pathetic lamentations. The birds seem to have been worshiped, or at least treated with the utmost care and respect. The Indians, besides their hunting and fishing, carried on a sort of trade with their neighbors of the mainland in small native tubers, called gicamas, with which the island abounded. They and their neighbors of the Santa Barbara channel were more advanced in the arts of life and more affable and agreeable than the other Indians of California.

From Santa Catalina, Viscaino passed to several of the neighboring islands and thence to the mainland near Point Concepcion. There he was visited on his ship by an Indian chief or head of a rancheria, whom he supposed to be king of the country. This chief appeared anxious to induce the Spaniards to land and was even supposed, like the chief with whom Drake treated at Point Reyes, to offer them his country and its sovereignty. Another of his offers was to give each one of the Spaniards, that would remain, ten wives who would work for and wait upon him. The proposition occasioned much merriment among the soldiers and sailors; but Viscaino did not think proper to accept the proffered hospitalities, and sailed on. Passing around Point Concepcion and running up the coast, he, on December 15, 1602, arrived at Point Pinos and came to anchor in the bay formed by its projection. Upon examination he found it a good port, with a pleasant and fertile neighborhood; and, on account of these advantages and in honor of the viceroy, under whose auspices he sailed, he gave it the name of Monterey.

By this time he found himself in very straightened condition. Many of his people were sick and his provisions

nearly exhausted.   He therefore deemed it prudent to send
back one of his vessels for the purpose not only of carrying
the invalids but also of soliciting reinforcements and procuring supplies.   As soon as it was gone, he and those who
remained with him fitted up barracks on shore and busied
themselves in furnishing the ships with wood and water.
They also set up a kind of chapel under an immense oak-
tree, whose spreading branches almost overhung the beach
and by the roots of which flowed abundant springs.   The
aspect of the country was delightful.   He and his men made
a short excursion inland and found the plains full of game—
elks, whose horns measured three yards across, deer, hares,
rabbits, geese, ducks and quails, besides other beasts and
birds in great numbers.   There were also bears, the prints
of whose feet were nine inches broad.   Throughout the
country there were numerous Indians, but they were all
friendly and well disposed.

On January 3, 1603, he set sail again with two vessels
and proceeded in search of Cape Mendocino.   A favorable
wind drove him up to the neighborhood of Point Reyes; but
there a storm came on, which separated the ships; and they
did not meet again until after the end of their respective
voyages.   Viscaino in his ship seems to have anchored, until the storm had somewhat abated, either in Drake's bay
or some one of the indentations of the coast near Point
Reyes.   He then sailed northwest again and on January 12
arrived off Cape Mendocino.   There the storm, coming on
with redoubled fury, lashed the sea into foam; and the mists
and clouds, settling down, shut out the view of earth and
sky and covered everything with murkiness and obscurity.
Only two of his sailors remained well enough to climb the
shrouds; and his ship was driven through the darkness, almost at the mercy of the raging elements, until he reached
latitude 42° north.   His experience of those stormy waters

was similar to that of Drake and Ferrelo. On January 20, the wind shifting to the northwest and the weather clearing up, he was in sight of Cape Blanco; but there, finding it impossible on account of the condition of his crew to proceed any further, he turned round and, running down the coast, on March 21, 1603, arrived at Acapulco.

The other vessel, which had separated from Viscaino at Point Reyes, was under command of Martin de Aguilar. It appears to have been driven northward to about latitude 43°, where, finding what appeared to be the mouth of a large river, Aguilar attempted to run in, but was prevented by the strength of the current. This supposed river he seems to have regarded as the western entrance of the straits of Anian, which was said to lead up past the city of Quivira into the Atlantic; and some geographers of subsequent years so delineated it on their maps under the name of the river of Martin de Aguilar. Instead, however, of sailing into and determining the truth in reference to the river, if he found one, Aguilar appears to have at once turned round and sailed with the news of his discovery for New Spain. His ship reached the port of Navidad on February 26, nearly a month before Viscaino reached Acapulco; but Aguilar himself, his chief pilot and most of his companions died on the passage.

Upon his return to Mexico, Viscaino made a full and minute report of what he had seen in California and particularly at Monterey, and solicited an opportunity of returning with sufficient and proper supplies and making a permanent settlement. Being referred for an answer to the king, he went to Spain, and for a long time endeavored in vain to interest the court in his project for another and better prepared expedition. But while he had a heart for battling against the tempests of the sea, he became discouraged in struggling against the neglect and slights to which he was subjected at Madrid, and returned disappointed to New Spain, with the intention of spending the rest of his days in retirement. Hardly, however, had he reached the retreat he sought, when the king, Philip III., on August 19, 1606, issued two cédulas or mandates, one directed to the viceroy of New Spain and the other to the governor of the Philippine islands, ordering a new expedition under the command of Viscaino for the occupation and settlement of Monterey, as a sort of half-way station between Mexico and Manila, for the benefit of the Philippine commerce. It may be imagined with what satisfaction the old navigator in his retirement heard of the new turn affairs had taken, and with what zeal he prepared to resume the labors of his youth. But, alas, his years were many; a life of toil and privation had made sad inroads upon his constitution; his strength was unequal to further efforts. He succumbed to his infirmities; and, as there was no one else to take his place, all prospects of carrying out the designs he had done so much to encourage and promote died with him.

SUGGESTIVE CORRELATIONS.

TO THE PUPIL.

1. What was the object of the first expedition of Viscaino? Of his second?
2. Make a list of the places touched by him off the coast of what is now California.
3. What island off the coast of California did he rename?
4. What rivers in the vicinity of Cape Blanco?
5. Can vessels at the present time ascend the rivers in that vicinity?
6. What was to have been the purpose of the third expedition by Viscaino?

CHAPTER XI.

The directions, given by Philip III., for a third voyage by Viscaino, provided, in the event of the death of that commander, that the enterprise should be prosecuted by his second in command. But these instructions were never carried into effect. The Philippine galleons still pursued their accustomed northern track; but nothing whatever was done to provide them stations, so much needed for refuge and supply, along the extensive line of coast from Cape Mendocino to Cape San Lucas. So far as that track extended northward, the sea had been carefully examined and mapped. But beyond, all was unknown. The voyage of Viscaino had not cleared up the vexed question in reference to the straits of Anian, while the report of his lieutenant Aguilar had left it in even greater uncertainty than before. All that was known was that there existed a vast region of deep ocean north of the parallel of Cape Mendocino; but so confused and contradictory were the accounts of it that it became a favorite region for writers of monstrous fictions. It was there that Lord Bacon located the scene of his New Atlantis; there too that Dean Swift fixed the country of his gigantic Brobdingnagians.

It is said that the Spaniards, after the discovery of the straits of Magellan, with the object of deterring other nations from sailing in that direction and interfering with their possessions on the new ocean, reported a swift and constant current sweeping from east to west through that passage,

(57)

which would easily drive vessels from the Atlantic into the Pacific, but would not admit of their return. This report was common in the time of Drake; but that bold navigator paid no attention to it, or, if he did, found that it was not true in fact. Cavendish also, as has been seen, followed Drake's track through the straits, and afterwards a number of other enemies of Spain took the same course. The Dutch especially—and particularly after their navigators Lemaire and Van Schouten had in 1616 opened the newer and more practicable route from ocean to ocean around Cape Horn— swarmed into the Pacific; and a portion of them, becoming corsairs and pirates, for a number of years infested the gulf of California. Choosing the western coast of New Spain as the safest theater of their depredations, they fixed their head-quarters in the bay of Pichilingue immediately north of La Paz—they themselves being called Pichilingues; and from there they made descents upon and devastated the exposed settlements to the southward.

After Viscaino, the first Spaniard, who sailed from New Spain for California, was Juan Iturbi. This was in 1615. He had two vessels, one of which was taken by the Dutch Pichilingues. With the other, he sailed up the gulf of California nearly to its head, and at various points stopped and collected pearls from the Indians. On his return as far as Sinaloa, he was ordered to join the then due Philippine galleon and protect it from the pirates, from whom it was in imminent danger. He accordingly ran across to Cape San Lucas; awaited the galleon, and convoyed it safely to Acapulco. Thence Iturbi proceeded to Mexico and threw that city into a state of great excitement by the exhibition of the pearls he carried with him. They were many in number and some very large and beautiful. One in particular was estimated to be worth nearly five thousand dollars—a sum of much greater value in those days than now. But most of his pearls were more or less damaged, owing to the fact that the Indians were accustomed to throw the unopened shells into the fire for the purpose of roasting the oysters.

The success of Iturbi induced many others to make expeditions to the gulf with the sole object of gathering pearls; and those who were most successful in plundering the I n d i a n s enriched themselves. These facts becoming known attracted public attention to the Californian pearl fisheries; and in a short time the Spanish government, seeing an opportunity of creating a new source of revenue, interfered and assumed control of them. Instead, however, of judiciously enco u r a g i n g private enterprise, such as might have led to the founding of stations and settlements, it imposed invidious restrictions and

PHILIP III., KING OF SPAIN.

[From " Los Gobernantes de Mexico."]

created a monopoly, which served to exclude colonists and effectually closed the country against immigration. This was the policy of Philip IV., who had succeeded to the Spanish throne in 1616; and there was no lack of competitors for the advantages expected to be derived from so rich and comparatively untouched a field. The most fortunate or adroit of these was Francisco de Ortega, who in due time received the royal license and set about preparing to enjoy the fruits of his monopoly.

Ortega sailed for California in 1632. He visited chiefly the coast between San Lucas and La Paz and collected pearls in large quantities. He made a second voyage in 1633 and another in 1634, and was successful in each. He appears to have been a man of considerable intelligence and urged upon the government the importance of occupying and permanently settling California. But while thus indulging in magnanimous projects, his chief pilot, one Estevan Carboneli, was secretly carrying on an underhanded negotiation on his own behalf with the viceroy of New Spain, the result of which was that Ortega lost the monopoly and Carboneli acquired it. Carboneli made a single voyage in 1636; but it was not remunerative; and, upon his return to Mexico, he fell into general and well-merited contempt.

The next of the pearl-fishers was Pedro Portel de Casanate. He succeeded, in 1640, in obtaining from the government a commission for the full exploration of the gulf of California, together with the exclusive privilege of navigating and trading in its waters. He was unable, however, on account of various obstacles, to get ready for his voyage before 1648, when he sailed with two vessels and made a complete round of the gulf. But he found nothing to justify his expectations and, returning a disappointed man, abandoned his monopoly and all rights and privileges connected with it. He was followed by Bernardo Bernal de Piñadero, who sailed in 1664. Piñadero devoted himself exclusively to the collection of pearls and exercised great tyranny and cruelty against the Indians, whom he compelled to dive and fish for him. His outrages became at length so intolerable that the Indians rose in revolt; and there was such frequent bloodshed that he soon found it prudent to return to Mexico with the booty he had managed to collect. He made a second voyage in 1667; but it was a failure. In 1668, Francisco Luzenilla received a license and made a voyage; but he also became involved in difficulties with the Indians, originating probably in the memory of the oppressions of Piñadero; and, after a number of vain efforts to establish peaceable relations, he too abandoned the monopoly and left the pearl-fisheries open to the small unlicensed adventurers from the opposite shores of Sinaloa.

SUGGESTIVE CORRELATIONS.

TO THE PUPIL.

1. Were the directions of Philip III., for the third expedition of Viscaino, carried out?
2. Why was the route from the Atlantic to the Pacific around Cape Horn regarded as more practicable than that through the Straits of Magellan?
3. When the Oregon was sent from Puget Sound to the Atlantic to take part in the war with Spain, did it go through the straits or around the Horn?
4. What business was the outgrowth of the voyage of Juan Iturbi up the Gulf of California in 1615?
5. Why did the Spanish government interfere with its development by private enterprise?
6. What was the result of the interference—1. As to the business? 2. Upon the country?
7. Of the men engaged in the trade, who seems to have been the most honorable?
8. Who was the king of Spain at that time?
9. Is the same business still carried on in the Gulf of California?
10. If so, state what you can learn about it.

CHAPTER XII.

ADMIRAL ATONDO.

CHARLES II., KING OF SPAIN.

[From "Los Gobernantes de Mexico."]

The ill-success of the last-mentioned pearl-fishing expeditions rendered the monopoly valueless. No one wanted it. Such being the case in 1677, and the importance of maintaining some kind of a Spanish force in California being recognized, Charles II., the then king, ordered an expedition for the final and permanent settlement of the country at the cost of the crown. This, in 1679, was committed to the charge of Isidro Atondo y Antillon, commonly known as Admiral Atondo, who at once began to furnish vessels, collect soldiers and colonists and provide stores for the proposed colonization. In the days of Cortés three or four months would have sufficed to complete all necessary arrangements for such an undertaking; but now it required three or four years.

Atondo sailed from the port of Chacala on March 18, 1683. He had two well-provided ships and over a hundred

(62)

men. He was accompanied by three Jesuit priests, the chief
of whom was the celebrated Father Kühn, a German, better
known by his Spanish appellation of Eusebio Francisco Kino.
In fourteen days he reached La Paz; but he found the place
abandoned by the natives, except a few armed and painted
bands, who manifested great ill-will and indicated by signs
that they wished the unwelcome visitors to leave. After
forming an encampment, and building a fort, church and
huts, Atondo made several excursions in the neighborhood.
He found the country to the eastward of La Paz very rough
and sterile and inhabited by an apparently weak and inof-
fensive race of Indians called Coras; but towards the westward, where the land was more level and less rocky, the
Indians, who were called Guaycuros, were fierce and very
hostile. They were also as active and enterprising as they
were hostile. Seizing their arms, they posted themselves in
a position to use them effectually if a safe opportunity should
present itself; and at the same time they secretly despatched
a party of their dusky warriors upon a rapid march to the
camp, in hopes of finding it sufficiently unprotected to justify
an attack. The Spaniards, however, were on their guard;
and for the time no assault was attempted.

This spirit of hostility on the part of the Guaycuros, notwithstanding repeated efforts to conciliate them, increased
rather than diminished. They endeavored for some time to
drive away the Spaniards by threats and warlike demonstra-
tions; and, when these failed, they collected in two large armed
bodies and with violent outcries advanced upon the camp.
As they approached, the Spanish soldiers ran to their de-
fenses; but the intrepid Atondo, choosing different tactics,
threw himself in front of the approaching savages and, with
terrific yells and assumed fierceness, challenged the entire
multitude to come on. Such gallant bravery was too much
for the Indian warriors; such a voice as that of Atondo

they had never before heard; such a fearful spectacle of fury
and wrath as he presented they had never before seen.   They
were paralyzed with astonishment; and, as Atondo advanced,
they precipitately turned their backs and fled in disorder.
Thus was the battle fought and won, like some of those de-
picted in Homer, by mere strength of lungs and show of rage.

But the Spanish did not long enjoy the fruits of their
easy victory.   A short time afterwards a mulatto boy mys-
teriously disappeared from camp and, it being reported that
the Guaycuros had murdered him, Atondo seized their chief
man and held him in custody.   The Indians immediately
collected in great numbers and demanded his release.   Being
refused, they joined all their forces and resolved to make
a general assault.   Atondo, more perhaps for the purpose
of inspiring his men with confidence in their means of de-
fense than with any purpose of slaughter, had caused a cannon to be loaded and pointed in the direction whence the
Indians approached; and then he and the Jesuit fathers went
round among the soldiers endeavoring to encourage them
to stand up against the savages and drive them off.   But on
every side they found nothing but cowardice and consterna-
tion.   With better material, there would have been no necessity for firing the gun; but under the circumstances no
other course seemed open; and as the Indians came on, the
cannon was discharged into their midst.   Ten or a dozen
were killed; many others wounded, and the rest were so
horror-stricken that they betook themselves to the mountains, glad to find any escape from the terrible engine of
destruction, which had thus been brought into requisition
against them.

It was evident from this experience that the Spaniards
could not anticipate peaceful intercourse with the Guaycuros;
and it was resolved to remove the settlement further up the
gulf shore.   The spot finally chosen was a place they called

San Bruno, about ten leagues north of Loreto. There, on October 6, 1683, they disembarked and, as at La Paz, proceeded to form a camp and build a fort, church and huts. They found the Indians, who had apparently never been much harassed by the pearl-fishers, quiet and peaceable; and for upwards of two years, during which the Spaniards remained, there does not appear to have been any serious disagreement or disturbance. While Atondo and his soldiers set themselves to exploring the country and attending to the temporal wants of the establishment, Father Kino and his associates were active in cultivating the friendship of the Indians, acquiring their language and converting them to the Christian faith.

It was at San Bruno, in the course of his missionary labors there, that Father Kino hit upon his famous method of teaching an ignorant people the doctrine of the resurrection. He could find nothing in their vocabulary to express the notion of resuscitation from death, and for a long time was at a loss to make them comprehend an idea so foreign to their modes of thought. He finally took several flies; put them in water until they were to all appearance dead; then took them out, covered them lightly with ashes and placed them in the sun. After a short exposure to the solar rays, the insects began to recover their vitality and, in a few moments, emerged, shook the ashes from their wings and flew away. The Indians, marveling at what had probably never before attracted their attention, exclaimed, "Ibimuhueite, Ibimuhueite." This word the fathers wrote down and thenceforth made use of, for want of a better, to signify the resurrection of Jesus Christ and to teach the seraphic life after death of those that believe in him.

Under the teachings and ministrations of a preceptor so skilful, as this little incident indicates Father Kino to have been, the Indians progressed rapidly. Within a year there were more than four hundred catechumens ready for baptism.   But their final admission into the bosom of the church, except in cases of approaching death, was delayed on account of the uncertainty felt by the fathers as to whether the establishment would be permanent.   As a matter of fact, it was soon ascertained that it would not be.   The country was found barren and unproductive; for a period of

eighteen months there had been no rain; there was . difficulty in procuring supplies, all of which had to be purchased and brought from across the gulf; there was much sickness; and, though the fathers urged that the next season might be better and that a further t r i a l should be made, Atondo resolved to break up camp and abandon the settlement.   He a c c o r d - ingly embarked all his people and returned to Mexico, after spending three years of time and laying out two hundred and twenty-five thousand dollars of the royal moneys without effect.   And such was the last attempt worthy of notice, under the direct auspices of the government, to colonize Lower California. Its ill-success rendered the supposition very general that the difficulties to be encountered were insuperable.   Though the protection of the Philippine ships and the interests of commerce required the occupation of the northwest coast as much or even more than at any previous time, its accom-

plishment seemed more and more improbable. But the
obstacles, which the Spanish crown could not surmount, the
Spanish church was equal to; and, as will be seen in the
sequel, the cross prevailed where the sword had failed.

SUGGESTIVE CORRELATIONS.

TO THE PUPIL.

1. What interests required the occupation of the northwest
   coast?
2. What was the object of the expedition of Admiral Atondo?
3. At whose expense was it fitted out?
4. When and from what port did the Admiral sail? Locate on
   the map facing page 6, the place from which he sailed.
5. Locate Loreto on the map facing page 6.
6. What method did Father Kino take to teach the Indians
   the doctrine of the resurrection?
7. What do you understand the word "catechumen" to mean?
   After you have a thorough understanding of its meaning,
   from having looked it up in Webster's "International
   Dictionary" or some equivalent work, use it in a sentence
   of your own.

GENERAL REVIEW.

1. What nation first reached India by sailing east? By sailing west?
2. Of what task was Spain relieved in 1492?
3. What work did she enter upon in 1570?
4. What effect had each upon her exploring and colonizing
   activity?
5. Make a list of her colonial possessions when at the height
   of her power. Tell why she does not possess them now,
   and when she ceased to do so.
6. By whom, and when, was the Spanish supremacy established in the Philippine islands?

7. If Lower California were still a part of California, who would have been the first Californian pioneer?
8. What was the object of the expedition of Cabrillo? Under whose direction did he undertake his explorations? Of what nationality was he? From what port did he sail? What had been the highest point on the Pacific Coast previously reached by the Spaniards? When did he discover the port now called San Diego? What did he name it? When did he discover Monterey Bay? How near did he come to discovering San Francisco Bay? When and where did he die? Where was he buried?
9. Who, as chief pilot, succeeded Cabrillo in command of the expedition?
10. When did the chief pilot discover Cape Mendocino? After whom did he name it?
11. What prominent cape did he discover on March 1, 1543?
12. To whom belongs the credit of the discovery of Alta California, or what we now term California?
13. To whom belongs the credit of sailing along its entire coast and ascertaining its general shape and character?
14. What do you see in the character of Cabrillo worthy of imitation? In that of his chief pilot?
15. Why do you suppose that the chief pilot missed seeing San Francisco Bay?
16. How many navigators on the Californian coast passed San Francisco bay and did not discover it? Name them.

MEMORIZE.

California was discovered at La Paz, Lower California, in 1534 by Fortuño Ximenez.

The first attempt to settle California was made by Cortés in May, 1535, at La Paz, or, as named by him, Santa Cruz.